FLY FIS

the
Bighorn
River

Hatches, Fly Patterns, Access, and Guides' Advice

Steve Galletta
Foreword by Pat Dorsey

Jim—
To trout filled days on the Bighorn!

HEADWATER
BOOKS

STACKPOLE
BOOKS

To all the anglers—family, friends, and clients—
with whom I have spent so many enjoyable hours on the water.

Copyright © 2015 by Headwater Books, LLC and Steve Galletta

Published by
HEADWATER BOOKS
PO Box 202
Boiling Springs, PA 17007
www.headwaterbooks.com

STACKPOLE BOOKS
5067 Ritter Road
Mechanicsburg, PA 17055
www.stackpolebooks.com

Printed in The United States of America

10 9 8 7 6 5 4 3 2 1

First edition

Cover design by Caroline Stover
Cover images by Pat Dorsey, Jay Nichols, and Paul Ruhter
Photos by the author except where noted

LOC Control #2015940064

ISBN 978-1-934753-34-7

CONTENTS

ACKNOWLEDGMENTS

I would first like to thank all of the fly-fishing writers that have contributed to the sport to which I have chosen to dedicate my life. The knowledge of fly fishing that can be gained by studying the words contained within the vast library of angling books over the past half century is astonishing.

On a personal level, I would like to thank my father for introducing me to the art of fly fishing and providing me with ample time on the water throughout my life.

I would also like to thank Hale Harris, who has always led by example. His mentorship and photographic contributions to this book have been invaluable. To Dr. Brad Harlan for his friendship on the water and his guidance and motivation throughout the book-writing process. To Jay Nichols for access to his abundant wealth of knowledge of photography and writing, and his dedication to making me perform at the best of my ability. To Pat Dorsey for his contribution as a mentor, and for showing me that a little hard work and dedication goes a long way in the fly-fishing business.

I don't think a woman truly understands what they are getting themselves into when they marry a fishing guide. For that reason I would like to thank my wife, Laurie, for her patience, support, and understanding over the years.

Last but not least, thanks to all that I have shared time on the water with in a professional and personal capacity.

FOREWORD

I made my inaugural trip to the fabled Bighorn River in the early 1990s. This was about a decade after it re-opened to the angling public in August 1981. Back then, I believed the "Horn" was arguably one of the finest trout streams in the United States. Nearly twenty-five years later, the Bighorn River still remains in a league of its own when it comes to America's best trout streams.

It didn't take me long to figure out that there was something special about the Bighorn River. The 13-mile stretch between Yellowtail Afterbay Dam and Bighorn Access is classic tailwater, providing anglers with a reliable four-season fishery, consistent flows, clear water, dependable hatches, and large populations of trout. Make no mistake about it—the Bighorn River is not your typical tailwater. It undoubtedly has more trout per mile than your average tailrace, better hatches, superb dry-fly fishing, and miles of public access to spread out the fishing pressure. Plus, as an added bonus, all the trout are wild as the Montana Department of Fish, Wildlife & Parks (FWP) does not conduct any artificial stocking of streams in Montana. This in itself makes the Bighorn unique among the top tailwaters in the country.

Tailwater junkies from all over the lower forty-eight gravitate toward the small community of Fort Smith, Montana, to fulfill their bucket list. The Bighorn Mountains provide a stunning backdrop as the river flows from the base of the dam through the Crow Indian Reservation, carving its way through rolling hills, buttes, and rich ranchland. The river is comprised of prime trout habitat including riffles, runs, pools, mid-channel shelves, point bars, back eddies, and back channels. Certain sections of the river are reminiscent of a Montana spring creek, while other stretches look and feel more like a typical cottonwood-lined freestone.

According to Montana FWP, the first 13 miles below the Yellowtail Afterbay Dam is home to 8,000 fish per mile. More than half of those fish are "young of the year" (fish under 7 inches in length), which proves the Bighorn's recruitment of wild fish is as good as it gets anywhere in the Western United States. Anglers will find a mixed bag of both browns and rainbows, with brown trout averaging 14 to 16 inches making up most the biomass. While the rainbows are fewer in number, they are consistently bigger, averaging 15 to 17 inches in length. It is important to note the biomass fluctuates annually based on the yearly snowpack and current water storage in Yellowtail Reservoir. The brown trout tend to favor higher flows whereas the rainbows tend to propagate better during lower flow regimes.

The Bighorn River caters to anglers who enjoy fishing with a wide range of tactics and techniques. Day in and day out, a skilled nymph-fisherman will consistently fool trout with a smorgasbord of subsurface offerings. During a hatch, the dry-fly fishing in and around the Fort Smith area is as good as it gets anywhere in the country. Toss in dependable streamer fishing and you have a world-class fishery.

I don't pretend to be an expert on the Bighorn River. It takes someone who spends hundreds of days each season on a particular watershed to become a true authority on a particular drainage. I can tell you this, however: the Bighorn River is a traditional Western tailwater that is extremely predictable. Tailwaters throughout the United States share many similarities with regard to matching the hatch, fly selection, seasonal strategies, reading the water, and the tactics and techniques required to fool the selective trout that live in the reaches below the dam. As a general rule, if you're successful on one tailwater, you should be successful on all tailwaters.

Furthermore, there is no substitution for time on the water if you want to become a proficient angler. Fly fishing is a continual learning endeavor for all levels and abilities. There is a strong correlation between knowledge

The Bighorn River has long been known for yielding trophy trout. JAY NICHOLS

Anglers come together year after year on the Bighorn for the consistent fly-fishing opportunity it provides. With abundant access, above average fish per mile, and excellent insect emergences the Bighorn produces excellent angling opportunity. HALE HARRIS

and success. The more you know about the river, the fish, matching hatches, choosing the appropriate flies based on the prevailing conditions, understanding seasonal strategies, and executing the correct techniques, the better chances you have of success.

Fly Fishing the Bighorn River will shorten your learning curve and provide valuable insight on fishing one of the greatest trout streams in the United States. Steve Galletta is a true authority on the river, and his in-depth knowledge will enhance your time on the water and provide you with a wealth of information that will increase your catch every time you fish the Bighorn.

Galletta's thorough discussions of hatches, fly selection, access points, and effective strategies to fool selective trout are the backbone of this book. His time-tested methods for success and other information come from spending nearly twenty years on the Bighorn, both personally and professionally as a guide. I am confident that this book will help you take your Bighorn experience to the next level. This book is a must-have reference for any serious angler's library.

Pat Dorsey
Parker, Colorado, 2015

INTRODUCTION

The Bighorn River is a complex and intricate trout fishery that has earned its world-class reputation over a relatively short period of time. Thriving populations of hard-fighting rainbow and brown trout have created a place of prominence among anglers around the world since the river was officially opened to angling in 1981, coincidently the year I was born.

Other than Idaho's Henry's Fork or Montana's Missouri River, I do not know of another river that offers hatches as consistent or as long in duration as the Bighorn. With excellent aquatic and terrestrial insect hatches from March through November, the Bighorn River offers anglers exceptional opportunities for match-the-hatch dry-fly fishing. While the insects found on the Bighorn River are small, their sheer abundance and the lengthy duration of their seasonal emergences create some of the most prolific dry-fly fishing in the West. The Bighorn's unique spring creek characteristics and highly conditioned trout demand the most from a dry-fly angler. The river's remarkable populations of brown and rainbow trout feed freely on these emerging insects, and the visual experience of both sight-nymphing to trout or casting to rising fish brings anglers back, year after year.

The one common thread between the people who choose to call the Bighorn Valley home and those who choose to visit each year is their love of the Bighorn River. While the makeup of the angling community that comes to this wonderful fishery is continually changing, I don't know of another river that provides anglers of every skill level with so much satisfaction. The beauty of the Bighorn is that anglers of all skill levels who enjoy fishing with a wide variety of techniques, such as nymphs, dry flies, and streamers, can find a rewarding fly-fishing experience on it. It will challenge the most seasoned of anglers, yet quickly gratifies those with little or no experience casting a fly—beginning anglers who experience fly fishing for the first time on the Bighorn are often spoiled for life. The Bighorn River has produced lasting memories for myself and the countless others who fish its waters each year. Regardless of your skill level, approaching the river with an open mind and immersing yourself in the many facets of this diverse fishery, in my opinion, is the key to any

The Bighorn River and its environs seem encapsulated in time. Anglers flock to the river, not only because of the world-class fishing, but also because of the experience it provides and the people that call it home. The Bighorn Valley has remained relatively unchanged, and anglers here today can have the same experience as in decades past. HALE HARRIS

angler's success. It is a complex trout fishery that will continue to challenge you throughout your evolution as an angler.

The Bighorn River, loved by many for its fantastic fly-fishing opportunities, handles angling pressure better than any river I know. Because of the sheer number of fish per mile and numerous miles of trout water, angler satisfaction on the Bighorn is as high as ever. For many, fly fishing is high church and the river is a place for solace and escape, a place in which anglers can immerse themselves in an experience that produces a greater sense of place and self. For me, a day on the river is not about the number of fish I can put in the net, but rather a time to immerse myself in an experience that allows me to gain a deeper understanding and appreciation for trout and the environs in which they live. The journey of fly fishing, not just on any given day but throughout your life, is valued in pursuing trout with a fly. Fisheries such as the Bighorn that produce

While the Bighorn has gone through many changes since officially opening to angling in 1981, a new generation of fly fishers can still find blue-ribbon trout fishing on the river.
JAY NICHOLS

experiences that we all greatly covet are a privilege that we all share in preserving for future generations.

I hope this book will increase the knowledge level of those anglers who have been fishing the Bighorn for many years and encourage those who have never fished the Bighorn to plan a trip. I also hope this book will stimulate Bighorn anglers to take a more active role in the stewardship of the river, by joining one, or all, of the organizations that work to preserve and enhance the Bighorn fishery.

The Bighorn River has provided me with much more than the simple enjoyment of fishing. It has provided me with a sense of place and self, a place to call home, and most of all, a higher calling in this life—introducing others to the art of fly fishing and the greatest trout river in the world, the Bighorn.

CHAPTER 1

Bighorn River Overview

To most, the Bighorn River starts in Fort Smith, Montana, right below Afterbay Dam, where the cool, bottom-release flows create ideal, year-round trout habitat. As anglers step into the cold, trout-laden water at Afterbay Access, they are often unaware that the Bighorn River has completed approximately two-thirds of its journey to the Yellowstone River, and that before reaching the trout mecca of Fort Smith, the Bighorn made its way hundreds of miles from the high peaks of Wyoming to the foothill plateaus surrounding Fort Smith. Originating in the Wind River Mountain range of western Wyoming, the Bighorn begins as a small mountain stream known as the Wind River. A number of other small streams add to it along the way as it flows mostly east, adding to its volume.

Just north of the town of Riverton, Wyoming, the Wind River flows into Boysen Reservoir, which is held back by Boysen Dam, one of three Bureau of Reclamation dams found in the Bighorn River system. Lake levels in Boysen Reservoir and outflows from Boysen Dam have a significant impact on flows into and out of Bighorn Lake each year.

At Boysen Reservoir, the Wind River turns north and flows through the geologically spectacular Wind River Canyon, a narrow gorge roughly fifteen miles long. When it exits the canyon, it reaches Wedding of the Waters. Contrary to the name, there are no other waters at this point. The Wind River only changes names as it leaves the canyon and is now the Bighorn River. From Wedding of the Waters, the Bighorn River flows north past the towns of Thermopolis, Greybull, Worland, Basin, and Lovell, Wyoming.

Just outside of Lovell, the Bighorn River enters Bighorn Canyon, home to the 72-mile Bighorn Lake. Also entering Bighorn Lake near Lovell is the Shoshone River, which drains a large corner of northwest Wyoming. The North Fork and South Fork of the Shoshone enter Buffalo Bill Reservoir west of Cody. The lake level of Buffalo Bill Reservoir and its outflows from the Shoshone River entering Bighorn Lake are also significant to the health of the Bighorn River fishery in Montana.

The Bighorn River tailwater fishery features near perfect trout habitat. Stable flows and optimal water temperatures created by the bottom release from Yellowtail Dam on Bighorn Lake provide exceptional angling opportunities throughout the year. These cold, clear, nutrient-rich flows produce a thriving biomass of insects and crustaceans that allow the abundant rainbow and brown trout to thrive. HALE HARRIS

Bighorn Lake is a geological wonder and is the heart of the Bighorn River trout fishery, providing the water that feeds the river all year.

During certain times of the year, the Bighorn River stretch from Wedding of the Waters through the town of Thermopolis is a good tailwater fishery. JAY NICHOLS

Cutting a giant chasm between the Pryor and Bighorn Mountain ranges, and navigable only by boat, Bighorn Canyon is a beautiful area. Bighorn Canyon, with Bighorn Lake contained therein, is home to black bears, mountain goats, wild horses, and other wildlife, along with a wide array of fish species. Bighorn Lake offers tremendous sportfishing opportunity for smallmouth bass, walleye, carp, brown trout, and rainbow trout. A boat is necessary when fishing Bighorn Lake because of the high canyon walls and the fact that there is only one access in Montana— Okabeh Marina, which is maintained by the National Park Service. It is becoming increasingly popular to fish in and around the marina from a drift boat. Fly fishermen will be greeted by world-class carp and smallmouth bass fishing, along with a chance at a trophy trout. The best fishing of the year for fly anglers is during the cicada hatch, which happens each year in June. These large terrestrial insects bring 3- to 8-pound carp by the hundreds to the surface as well as the lake's largest trout that reach 28 inches in length. Opportunity on the lake continues throughout the summer when trout and carp can be found taking a variety of terrestrials from the surface. Anglers willing to strip streamers can find smallmouth bass willing to take their fly.

Bighorn Canyon ends at Yellowtail Dam. Finished in 1967, Yellowtail Dam is one of the tallest dams in the United States, standing 525 feet tall and 1,480 feet wide as it spans the mouth of the canyon. Before Yellowtail Dam, the Bighorn River was much warmer, often ran muddy in the spring and after rainstorms, and was subject to large and erratic fluctuations in water levels. It was home to warmwater species such as channel catfish, sauger, goldeye shad, and burbot (ling).

The waters of Bighorn Lake now flow out the bottom of Yellowtail Dam, pushing as many as four power turbines with the capacity to generate 250 MW of electricity for eastern Montana. This bottom-release flow is responsible for the cold, clear water that supports the Bighorn's amazing fishery throughout the year. Flowing to the northeast, through the lush agricultural land of the Bighorn Valley and the Crow Indian Reservation, a 2.3-million-acre reservation in southeast Montana, this well-known Montana stretch of the Bighorn River offers 35 miles of trout water that draws anglers from around the world.

Fort Smith

Named after Civil War general Charles Ferguson Smith, Fort C. F. Smith was erected in 1866 to protect travelers of the Bozeman Trail heading west to discover gold around Virginia City, Montana. Manned by the 18th Infantry and the 27th Infantry, the fort remained operable for only two short years until it was decommissioned and abandoned in 1868.

The Bighorn Valley offers a splendid backdrop for a day of fishing. Traveling through this agricultural valley is like taking a step back in time, as ranchers and farming families keep the traditions of Montana alive.

Today, the National Park Service grants much of the access surrounding Fort Smith.
ASHLEY GARRISON

Fort Smith took on new meaning in 1961, when the construction of Yellowtail Dam began. In addition to the infrastructure created by the federal government on nearby federal lands, Fort Smith provided local amenities to dam workers from 1961–1967. Once the dam was complete and the lake was filled with water by 1967, the massive bottom-release dam produced near-perfect conditions for trout in the river downstream of it. Realizing the potential of the newfound conditions of the Bighorn River, Montana fisheries managers stocked trout in the river in 1966 and continued through the late 60s. These original trout quickly thrived in the clear, cold flows of the newly created Bighorn River. By the early 70s, Fort Smith, by way of people in the know, became a jumping-off point for those looking to fish the Bighorn River.

Contained within the confines of the Crow Indian Reservation, anglers gained access to the river by purchasing a permit from the tribe. This access, however, proved to be relatively short-lived. As popularity of the resource increased, so did conflicts between anglers and tribal members. As a result, the tribe voted to close the Bighorn River to angling by all non-Native Americans in May 1974. Shortly after the closure, the Bureau of Indian Affairs arrested a trespassing angler on the river and confiscated his gear. This arrest was the catalyst for a six-year court battle between the state of Montana and the Crow Tribe, who were represented by the United States. This case over who had governing jurisdiction over these waters was finally adjudicated in 1981. The Supreme Court sided with the state of Montana, based on the law that access to navigable waters was held by the state and therefore the fishing rights were held by the state of Montana as well.

After the Supreme Court's decision, Montana Department of Fish, Wildlife & Parks (FWP) began a two-year impact and fishery study of the resource to determine trout populations, bag limits, and how to manage the fishery as a whole. On August 1, 1981, the Bighorn River opened to angling, and anglers were greeted by a trout fishery unlike any other in the world. According to longtime Bighorn River outfitter Ritchie Montella, "In 1982 I caught 96 fish between 4$\frac{1}{2}$ and 8 pounds, mostly on dry flies."

In spring 1982 Mike Craig opened the Bighorn Angler, the first full-time fly shop in Fort Smith. Over the course of a few short years, the Bighorn River and the small community of Fort Smith, made up mostly of fishing guides and others who provide services for traveling anglers, turned into a worldwide destination for fly fishermen. Today, multiple year-round full-service fly shops and lodges serve the needs of anglers. In addition to these local businesses, where anglers can book guided trips, buy supplies, and rent drift boats, anglers will find a small market with fuel pumps, a few local restaurants, a laundromat, and a post office.

People don't happen upon Fort Smith. There is only one way in and one way out, and other than the river itself, there isn't much reason to venture this far south of Interstate 90. For those of us who call Fort Smith home and those that visit yearly, Fort Smith represents a gathering place for all who have a deep-rooted passion in life that reveals itself when casting a fly to rising trout in the clear waters of the Bighorn River.

A visit to Fort Smith should be seen as an added bonus to a trip to this world-class fishery. Fort Smith represents something different for everyone who visits. What you won't find in Fort Smith is bars (dry town), shopping, or five-star dining establishments. Instead, Fort Smith represents a slow-paced, laid-back atmosphere, free from many of the hindrances of highly developed cities. What you will find is easy access to world-class fishing and friendly individuals proud of their community who welcome fly fishers from around the world.

The Tailwater Ecosystem

The Bighorn River that we know today would not have been possible without the completion of the Yellowtail Dam, which created a flourishing river habitat that allows trout populations to thrive and provides an angler

Camping on the Bighorn

The Bighorn Valley supports the American tradition of camping and fishing as well as anywhere in Montana. Whether you are looking to pitch a tent or camp with the comfort of home from your RV, there are good options found throughout the area.

The National Park Service maintains two highly desirable campgrounds along the shore of Afterbay Lake. You will find one located on the west side of the lake and another on the east side only a few short miles from Fort Smith. Both are well maintained and have fire pits, bear boxes, picnic tables, vault toilets, and water. Both campgrounds are suitable for tent camping or RVing.

Camping or overnight parking is not permitted at Afterbay Access or Three Mile Access. However, you can find a nice area to tent camp or hook up a camper trailer at Cottonwood Campground (cottonwoodcampbighorn.com), located along the access road to Three Mile Access. In addition to campsites, Cottonwood Camp provides shower houses, bathrooms, laundry facilities, and a small store.

Moving downriver, a primitive campground can be found at Bighorn (Thirteen Mile), Access. This state campground contains a vault toilet, fire rings, and a little more solitude. A half mile south of Bighorn Access, located on Highway 313, you will find Garrison Stoker Resort (garrisonstokerresort.com), a well-maintained RV park. Each site has water hook-ups and 50-watt power supply for the largest RVs. This is also home of Tailwater Restaurant, which provides home-cooked meals for a moderate price.

Moving farther north, you will find one more primitive campsite at Mallard's Landing right along the river, once again containing fire rings and a vault toilet. ■

with exceptional year-round angling opportunities. Yellowtail Dam created Bighorn Lake, a 72-mile body of water that reaches depths of 400 feet. Dam managers have the ability to control, store, and manage outgoing flows from the dam based on the amount of inflow coming into Bighorn Lake at any given time. Snowpack in the mountains, air temperatures, and annual rainfall all affect the amount of inflow entering the Reservoir.

The relatively small, 2.2-mile Afterbay Dam acts as a buffer between Yellowtail Dam and the river. Water levels in the Afterbay can fluctuate up to 15 feet daily based on power demands and management of water levels in Bighorn Lake. The Afterbay also acts as a giant settling pond, allowing sediment and debris to settle out. As a result of the dam system, water enters the river clean and clear throughout the year.

Yellowtail Dam and the formation of Bighorn Lake turned the Bighorn River into a premier trout stream. Water storage of this capacity helps create ideal fishing conditions each year. In low-water years, we still have enough to maintain healthy minimum flows, and in high-water years, dam managers have the ability to store water and release flows in a controlled manner.

Afterbay Dam is the second of two dams below Bighorn Lake that are responsible for the highly prolific tailwater ecosystem below.

While water releases from Yellowtail Dam and Afterbay Dam vary seasonally, outflows into the river are always at a fishable level. I have seen outflows as low as 1,400 cfs and as high as 15,000 cfs and had great fishing at both levels, as well as everywhere in between. Any major water flow changes typically occur in the spring, due to runoff, and if water releases do need to rise, these increases happen in small stages, which doesn't disrupt the fishing.

Throughout the summer, flows typically remain constant, because precipitation is pretty low in the region. We may see small bumps in flows, signaled by a brief increase in aquatic vegetation and other debris, as dam managers maintain flows in the Afterbay.

Bighorn Lake, because of its size and depth, also mitigates wide variances in water temperature throughout the year. In general, because of the volume of water in Bighorn Lake, it takes longer for temperature changes to occur. Most importantly, water being released from the bottom of the dam remains cold when air temperatures are at their highest. When air temperatures reach the 80s and 90s consistently throughout the summer, water releases from Afterbay may still only be in the upper 40s or low 50s. In the fall, it takes water temperatures in the river a longer time to cool, especially compared to freestone rivers, because the lake retains its heat for a significant amount of time before cooling. This is why our mayfly and caddis hatches can last well into November—longer than most other rivers.

Water temperatures also dictate when fall turnover of the lake occurs. As air temperatures cool in the fall, so does the water on the surface of the lake. This layer of cold water on the surface becomes the heaviest and densest layer of the lake. Because of this, it sinks. When this happens, floating vegetation, debris, and anything else contained in the dense film goes to the bottom. Once on the bottom, this newly mixed water is released from the dam into the river. The timing of this turnover depends on the weather from one year to the next. This typically occurs in mid-October, but can take place through the end of November. In some years it

Afterbay Lake and Afterbay Dam are critical components of the Bighorn's tailwater ecosystem. After being released by the dam, this water flows into the Afterbay, a 2-mile reservoir created by the dam at the north end to absorb the fluctuating water releases from Yellowtail Dam, which change with hydroelectric needs. Afterbay Reservoir contributes to the stable flows in the river below Afterbay Dam.

is noticeable and other years it is not. In the worst of years, though rarely, the river looks like pea soup for miles and floating vegetation abounds. During a normal year, water will be slightly stained for a few miles and the fishing remains good.

During the winter, water temperatures remain warmer than other rivers and stay at a near constant temperature, which promotes optimal feeding conditions for trout and creates year-round angling opportunities. These relatively warm winter water temperatures also allow the river to remain ice free for many miles below the dam.

In addition to the cold, clean water that Bighorn Lake produces, the water contained within the lake is also incredibly nutrient rich. The limestone geology of Bighorn Canyon and the high rate of photosynthesis that occurs from prolonged exposure to sunlight produce a large quantity of phytoplankton, along with highly alkaline and mineral-rich water. This nutrient-rich water promotes the growth of the aquatic vegetation in the river that supports an aquatic biomass unlike anywhere else. This biomass consists of an inconceivable abundance of crustaceans, annelids, and aquatic insects that sustain the incredible trout populations found in the Bighorn.

While the aquatic insects found in the Bighorn, and other similar tailwater fisheries, are not large in size like on freestone rivers, their emergences are incredibly dense. In addition, the seasonal emergences of these insects are also much longer than on freestone rivers. The consistent nature of tailwater rivers, and the abundance of food they create, allows trout to feed, with relative ease, throughout the year. Because of this, trout populations on the Bighorn are high and trout grow at a fast rate, almost twice as fast as fish do in a typical freestone river.

Today, mostly due to angling pressure and consistently lower than average stream flows, the overall numbers of fish per mile and the average size of the trout are lower than when the river opened to public fishing in 1981. While this may be the case, the Bighorn River still supports a wild population of rainbow and brown trout that is higher than many of the other trophy trout rivers throughout Montana.

CHAPTER 2

Trout Species

Proponents of dam building always promote recreational opportunities as a byproduct of dam construction. In the case of the Yellowtail Dam, they couldn't have been more right. In 1966, Montana FWP introduced just over 9,000 rainbow trout to the Bighorn River for the first time. The Bighorn River, between 1966 and 1989, was stocked with numerous strains of rainbows to discover which one best adapted to the habitat. These strains included Arlee, Eagle, Shasta, and Desmet rainbow trout. It was the Desmet strain from nearby Lake Desmet in Wyoming that proved to be most successful because they were able to reproduce and spawn in the main river and side channels of the Bighorn, similar to spawning within a lake. These Desmet rainbows also successfully crossbred with the other species previously stocked in the Bighorn River. This spawning success led to incredible numbers of rainbow trout per mile and eventually to the end of the stocking program in the Bighorn River. Up through 1989, Montana FWP stocked the river with as many as 50,000 rainbow trout per year. By 1989, the Bighorn River maintained self-sustaining populations of rainbow and brown trout and has not been stocked since.

Due to years of stocking different strains of rainbows and the single introduction of cutthroat trout in 1972 (one batch of 12,000 Yellowstone cutthroat), rainbow trout in the Bighorn have evolved into a unique strain of the species. You won't find another rainbow trout like it anywhere else in the world. While far fewer cutthroats were stocked in the Bighorn than rainbows, this original hybridization of the two species is often present in the rainbow trout population that we find in the river today. Most of the river's rainbow trout have a distinct orange slash below their jaw line, prominent on pure-strain cutthroat. While rare, a rainbow in the Bighorn will even have spotting traits belonging to the cutthroat—fewer spots on the back and sides and more on the tail.

With no known stockings of brown trout into the Bighorn River by the state of Montana, brown trout on the Bighorn can be linked all the way

The cold, well-oxygenated water in the Bighorn is ideal for producing thick, hard-fighting rainbows such as this one ready for release. PAT DORSEY

back to their introduction by European settlers moving west. Originally cultivated by Seth Green in the late 1800s in Caledonia, New York, brown trout were often transported by rail car and dumped off of bridges, into rivers and streams, as the West expanded.

The brown trout found in the Bighorn River today either made their way into the river via rail car or found the river on their own, moving up from the Yellowstone, or down from a smaller tributary stream that they were released into by settlers. Brown trout have been wild and self-sustaining throughout their entire existence in the Bighorn River and were possibly residents of the river before the dam was built.

While Montana FWP lumps all brown trout together as the Loch Leven variety, from my experience, the trout that I encounter on the Bighorn depict dominant traits that most often resemble what I have come to know as those of the German brown trout species. I typically distinguish Loch Leven browns as having large, dark spots that are few in abundance and a lack of red spots. German brown trout typically have an abundance of fine spots, with many often red. It is my opinion that the majority of the brown trout population should be classified as the German brown trout.

Peak populations of wild trout occurred in 1994, with approximately 12,000 trout per mile in the upper river. During the Bighorn's lowest point, after several harsh drought years, populations dropped as low as 3,000 catchable fish per mile, still higher than just about any other trout river in Montana. Periods of drought are part of our reality in the West and have been cyclic in nature over the years. When trout populations in the river decrease, the benefit is that the average size of the fish in the river typically increases. When the number of fish per mile increases, the average size of the fish typically decreases. If you ask local anglers, many will tell you that they prefer fewer fish in the river, with a larger size on average. The upper river today, during a normal year, holds a healthy population of trout that averages 5,000 to 6,500 fish per mile, which provides anglers with plenty of fish to cast their flies to, along with a chance at some true trophies.

A river bottom made up of small to fine gravel and a relatively moderate flow produces high rates of successful spawn in the river's rainbow and brown trout, but populations vary, mostly due to cycles of high- and low-water years and other conditions that affect successful spawning.

Historical data suggest that low-water years favor a more successful spawning season for rainbows in the spring, and high-water years favor a better spawning season for brown trout in the fall. In 2005 and 2007, there

Brown trout are the dominant species in the Bighorn. They grow rapidly and take flies eagerly, making them great sport for anglers. JAY NICHOLS

Bighorn River rainbow trout spawn in the main river and side channels due to a lack of adequate tributaries. The river's fine gravel bottom is ideal for trout reproduction.
HALE HARRIS

was a near even split in the distribution of rainbows to browns. Most recently, in 2011, after four high-water years, the success of the brown trout spawn resulted in 74 percent of the river's trout population being brown trout. We expect the river's trout population to naturally balance itself out and for populations of brown and rainbow trout to be somewhere around a 60/40 split in favor of the brown trout.

While the population and distribution of the trout will fluctuate with varying river conditions from year to year, the average size of the fish has remained fairly consistent over the years. Because of the abundance of food, trout quickly grow to an average size of 15 to 16 inches within two years, weighing between 1½ and 2 pounds. Each year, the largest fish caught in the river typically ranges from 25 to 28 inches. While these trophies are few and far between, there are healthy populations of fish in the 20-inch range.

During consecutive low-water years, the average size of fish goes up to around 17 inches, mostly because of less competition with other trout. This is especially true for the river's rainbow trout during low-water years. In high-water years, the river in general sees higher populations of trout and brown trout in particular become more abundant. Because of this abundance, the size of the average fish goes down slightly to the 14- to 16-inch range.

Generally speaking, trout in the Bighorn grow at a rate twice as high as the same species of fish in freestone rivers. The enormous volume of aquatic insects in the river allows small trout to aggressively consume these various sources of energy, producing tremendous growth rates at a young age. Because these trout consume food so aggressively throughout their life and grow so quickly, their life span is often shorter than trout found in other rivers. Most Bighorn trout only live for four, maybe five, years before perishing due to the fast-paced environs in which they live.

Rainbow Trout

Rainbow trout are indigenous to the Pacific Northwest, where they evolved in the region's rough and tumble mountain rivers and streams. Rainbows in the Bighorn, much like all rainbow trout, are not as tolerant as brown trout when it comes to extremes in water temperatures. Rainbows prefer well-oxygenated, often faster water. The Bighorn is ideally suited to rainbows, running from 38 to 60 degrees in temperature throughout the year. During the coldest months, rainbows move to the slowest water they can find in the Bighorn. The opposite is true when water temperatures are at their highest during the summer; these rainbows will move to the fastest, most oxygenated water in the river to be comfortable. This can often be in less than two feet of water.

Certain runs are definitely more likely to hold rainbow trout rather than brown trout. These congregated populations of rainbows, found throughout the Bighorn, are most easily targeted with nymph imitations. Bighorn River rainbow trout are efficient feeders and even the largest rainbow trout in the Bighorn will feed on the abundance of subsurface food during their entire lives. Rainbow trout receive a larger proportion of their diet from the river's crustacean populations of scuds and sow bugs than brown trout.

Healthy, hard-fighting Bighorn River rainbow trout are what fly-fishing dreams are made of.
DAVID PALMER

Because of this characteristic, rainbow trout don't provide the best surface action; during match-the-hatch situations, you will predominantly catch brown trout. Rainbows become more susceptible on the surface when they feed opportunistically on larger attractors and terrestrial patterns. However, on any drift with a nymph, an angler can catch a true trophy of a rainbow. Once rainbows reach a larger size of around eighteen inches, these fish begin to more readily forage on other fish in the river and the river's larger rainbows readily take streamers.

Rainbow trout spawn in the spring, any time from late April through mid-June, depending on water temperatures. The ideal water temperature for successful rainbow spawn is in the low 50s. We typically see ideal water conditions and temperatures for the rainbow trout spawn in mid-May. These fish spawn in the river's numerous side channels, as well as in shallow riffles along the edges of the main river. It is unethical and damaging to the fishery to target spawning fish, and it is important to avoid walking through the light-colored gravel that has been cleared by rainbows to lay their eggs. During the spring, there is still a large population of fish not on spawning redds available to anglers.

Brown Trout

While the origin of brown trout species in the Bighorn River is unknown, both Loch Leven and German brown trout have thrived in the Bighorn since the completion of Yellowtail Dam. Brown trout, being the most adaptable and having the highest tolerance to varying river conditions,

This large brown was sight-nymphed in a shallow side channel riffle. AMBER GARRISON

Fall is a magical time to be on the Bighorn River. The vibrance of the season is found not only in the cottonwood set a blaze along the river's edge, but also in the brown trout that aggressively come to a fly. JAY NICHOLS

such as water flow, temperature, and water quality, are much more widespread throughout the river than rainbows. Brown trout can be found as far as 50 miles below the dam.

Browns throughout the country are known for being highly selective feeders and often one of the most difficult fish to catch with a fly. On the Bighorn, most of the browns are much more susceptible to a well-presented fly, though the largest trophy browns are difficult to fool. Catching a trophy brown trout is often a product of being in the right place at the right time. Many of the largest brown trout each year are found in deep holes throughout the river and occasionally leave themselves susceptible to the angler when they move into spots to feed that provide less shelter. I find that this happens more often than not on the lower river below Bighorn Access, where fishing pressure is significantly lower. In 2014, there were two very large browns, one of 25 inches and another of 27 inches, caught in the first 3 miles of the river on nymphs.

The abundant aquatic insects and optimal water conditions found in the upper 20 miles of the Bighorn create the best fishing opportunities for brown trout, because of their propensity to take a dry fly. The relatively slow and even flows of the Bighorn allow them to feed efficiently on the surface, which is why 90 percent of the trout you catch on the surface of the Bighorn will be brown trout.

Brown trout can be found in large pods feeding rhythmically and freely on all of the river's major insect hatches. Because of their propensity to feed on the surface and their ability to acclimate to a wide range of water temperatures, you will also find browns feeding on the surface nearly year-round, which is one of the attributes that sets the Bighorn apart from many other great trout rivers.

As fall arrives on the Bighorn, brown trout begin to show their vibrant spawning colors. The brown trout spawn on the Bighorn River happens later than on many other rivers across Montana, because the Bighorn's tailwater flows take much longer to cool each fall. While Bighorn brown trout start to show their spawning colors in September and early October, when browns would typically begin spawning on many Western freestone rivers, they won't be found on spawning beds until November and December.

Bighorn brown trout readily attack streamer patterns each fall as they forage on other fish and become increasingly territorial leading up to their spawn. This is some of the most exciting fishing of the year throughout the whole river and many anglers plan their annual trips around it.

Trout Behavior

All wild trout share a set of characteristics related to how they feed, defend themselves, and reproduce. Trout not only want to do all of these things successfully—they also want to do them efficiently. The larger and older fish become, the more efficient they become at evading predators and feeding, making them harder to be captured by anglers. The Bighorn River's habitat has shaped the way Bighorn trout behave. I am not a fish biologist, but after spending countless hours on the water, I have been able to distinguish certain tendencies in how Bighorn River trout behave.

An angler's approach and presentation should go hand in hand. At the foundation of your approach is understanding where and how trout feed. There are three main areas to cover when talking about how and where trout feed: opportunistic vs. selective feeding, subsurface and surface feeding, and river features that hold trout.

Opportunistic vs. Selective Feeding

When a trout feeds on any number of available food sources at a given time, rather than keying in on one thing, it is feeding opportunistically. Because of the sheer volume of food found in tailwater rivers, trout in them have a high propensity to feed opportunistically at any given time and are far less likely to have on-off periods of feeding activity.

Riffles such as this one located a few miles below the dam are ideal for finding opportunistically feeding fish. HALE HARRIS

Fish are going to feed opportunistically most often when feeding on or near the bottom, where at any time of the year there can be a variety of crustaceans and nymphs of mayflies, midges, and/or caddisflies. Any of these organisms can become dislodged and found in the drift. During periods of low insect activity, trout are also more likely to feed opportunistically because there is an absence of any one dominant food source.

Opportunistic feeding behavior lends itself to prospecting, or blind-fishing, for trout. This is why anglers fish the Ray Charles fly, in one form or another, every day of the year with such great success. Bighorn trout feed on sow bugs opportunistically, regardless of other available food sources in every type of water. When nymph fishing "turns off," or becomes slower for the angler, it is most often because the fish have started to focus on one predominant insect.

Opportunistic feeding on the surface happens far less than on other rivers because of the abundance of food in the Bighorn; these trout simply don't have to over-exert themselves to capture food, but when they do it is great sport. Terrestrials such as ants, beetles, and grasshoppers are often worth the fish's effort to move from the bottom of the river to the surface. I find that the trout in the lower river feed more opportunistically on the surface than the upper river, because of a lower density of aquatic insects.

Selective feeding occurs when there is an abundance of one food source or insect and the trout feed on it exclusively at a given time. Selective feeding can make the fishing more technical because there is less

Selectively feeding trout will often key in on one stage of an emergence when feeding on the surface or in the surface film.

room for error in your fly selection, but once you break the code, you can have terrific fishing. When selective feeding occurs subsurface, you might think the water is void of fish until you pick the right pattern. Remember that your fly selection is only as good as your presentation.

While selective feeding often occurs on the bottom of river, especially during a hatch, it is most evident when trout are feeding on, in, or below the surface film. The good thing is that when trout are feeding on the surface, they give you numerous clues as to what stage of a hatch they are feeding on. By reading the riseforms, observing what is flying in the air and what can be seen on the surface of the water, you can determine what the trout are feeding on.

The thing that makes fishing to feeding trout on the surface challenging is that these selective feeders not only key in on a particular insect but also a particular stage of the hatch cycle—cripples, floating nymphs, half-in/half-out emergers, and/or duns. The challenge of selecting the right pattern and hooking a selectively feeding trout on the surface is what dry-fly anglers often covet most and can be a source of great joy or frustration.

Feeding Zones

To break things down to the simplest root level, trout are either feeding on the bottom of the river or at the surface, and they are doing so opportunistically or selectively. In a few instances, they will be feeding in the middle of the water column.

On the Bighorn, trout consume almost all of their food (perhaps 90 percent) subsurface, mostly along the bottom. Because trout feed in this zone every day of the year, learning how to fish it effectively should be a high priority. During non-hatch periods of the year, fishing along the bottom with patterns that imitate annelids, scuds, sow bugs and larvae, pupae, and nymph forms of various aquatic insects is going to be your best option. The bottom of the river amongst the rocks offers trout both protection from predators and a current break in which they can efficiently hold. The fish will hold along the bottom in different water types, as conditions such as water levels and temperature change throughout the seasons and as different hatches occur. Your presentation, tactics, and rigging should change as the fish move into these different seasonal lies based on the depth of water and the speed of the current.

Catch-and-Release

Even though catch-and-release has become the norm among fly fishers today, post-release mortality is much higher than people think. Most mortality is not immediate either. Many of the fish will eventually die sometime after being released due to trauma incurred during their encounter with the angler. Properly fighting, landing, and handling the trout will ensure that the trout survives to be caught another day.

After hooking a fish, fight it as quickly as possible by applying significant pressure to the fish. When applying a proper amount of pressure, you should have a deep bend in your rod. Applying pressure at various angles will also help to quickly bring the trout to hand. I see far too many anglers standing in the river with the rod straight up and not stripping or reeling in any line. Overplaying your fish will result in a great amount of unnecessary stress to it.

When landing a fish, always try to use a net and always keep the fish in the water while handling it and removing the hook. "Beaching" your fish on the rocks is probably the worst thing you can do. After removing the hook, return the fish to the water in your net before removing it again to take a picture. The trout should be quickly taken from the water to remove the hook, then left in the water until the cameraman is ready to take the picture and you have the trout held properly for the photo. After capturing your photo, hold the trout in the river upstream until it is ready to swim away on its own power.

Use barbless hooks to protect the fish. They can be removed quickly, and they often back out of the trout's mouth on their own once a trout is in the net. Barbed hooks can often damage the trout's mouth. Maimed trout are far less pleasurable to catch a second time. This is most evident when Bighorn trout are missing their mandibles. ■

When we talk about the surface feeding zone, we really mean the surface film. Trout either feed on, in, or just below the surface film. When trout are feeding on the surface, they are both exposed and vulnerable to predation. Trout move to the surface simply to feed. These lies rarely provide shelter or protection, except for when they feed tight to the bank underneath cover. Trout are drawn to the surface to feed selectively, not only on a particular insect but, typically, a particular stage of an emergence. The surface film is where all the magic happens and probably the most dynamic aspect of a trout river and also one of the hardest concepts for new anglers to understand.

The surface film is actually scientifically defined as surface tension. When exposed to the air, water molecules have a greater attraction to each other, causing cohesion of the molecules, resulting in an effect that resembles the surface of the water being covered with a stretched elastic membrane. This layer is what anglers know as the surface film. The surface film of the river is only one molecule thick. This tension on the water's surface is what allows insects that are denser than water to float on the surface. This uppermost layer also acts as a barrier for emerging insects making their way to the surface. As insects struggle to break free through this barrier, they begin to collect in large quantities just below the surface film and become highly susceptible to the trout. Not only does the film collect emerging insects, it also traps spinners, egg-laying, and spent insects. Because of the diversity of insects found in the film, anglers can use numerous techniques to successfully capture feeding fish. Anglers can fish nymphs just below the surface film, swing wet flies through it, fish emergers in it, and fish dun or adult imitations on top of it.

Let's look at a few examples of how insect emergences on the Bighorn interact with the surface film. Because of their small size, midge pupae are more prone to having their emergence process impeded by the surface film of the river. Trout take advantage of this activity during every midge emergence. As an angler, it is deadly effective to trail a midge pupa imitation a short distance below a more visible dry fly, or hand twist a small wet fly just under the surface film, mimicking the struggling pupa as it squirms to break through the surface.

I find mayfly patterns to be the most effective flies to fish in the surface film. Because of their larger size, mayflies will often hang half in the surface and half on top as they break free from their nymphal shuck. Fishing a half-in/half-out imitation is deadly during a mayfly emergence and trout will key in on this characteristic frequently. The same is true of crippled mayflies and spinners that are trapped motionless in the surface film.

The adult stage of any insect hatch found on the Bighorn is susceptible to predation on the surface of the water. The more time an insect spends on the surface, the more susceptible it is to the trout. For example, a Blue-Winged Olive dun often floats on the surface of the water much longer than a Pale Morning Dun does because of colder air temperatures, making it more likely for trout to feed on the adult stage of the insect during a BWO hatch rather than a PMD hatch. Even more so than duns, spent spinners and spent caddis adults are that much more important to the trout, because there is no possibility of escape from these dead insects.

Where Trout Feed

While Bighorn trout use the entire river to hold and feed, there are several types of river features that consistently hold large populations of trout. Many of these lies provide ideal feeding stations for the trout. Trout move around to different feeding stations throughout the year, depending on water levels and, especially, water temperature. Each feature dictates a strategic approach—some are best approached as subsurface feeding zones and others as surface feeding zones.

DROP-OFFS AND SHELVES

As water plunges over rock, a large amount of food is dislodged from gravel and delivered efficiently to fish waiting below. Fish will sit in different parts of the shelf or drop-off, depending on water temperature or insect activity. Drop-offs and shelves can be easily identified by a distinct color change, typically from a clear, tan color created by the shallow water flowing over rock, to a deep green color represented by the deeper area on the downstream side of the drop-off.

A shelf such as this one is an ideal place to find an abundance of Bighorn trout. Food is efficiently delivered to their feeding lie. HALE HARRIS

Because of the number of trout per mile and the abundance of food in the Bighorn, don't overlook any water on the Bighorn; even the smallest drop-off or surface disturbance is an indicator of a trout lie. PAUL RUHTER

During an insect emergence, or during the heat of summer, fish will feed in the skinny riffle water above the drop-off, and right on the drop, intercepting insects in the drift. When the water is colder, fish will sit back away from the shelf, where the water is slower and easier to hold in. When fish are holding right below the drop, you want to have enough weight to get your flies down quickly immediately after the drop. Prime runs on the Bighorn that feature drop-offs and shelves are the Sandbar, Meat Hole, Dag's Run, Graycliff Shelf, and Craig's Shelf.

FLATS

These are probably the most overlooked areas by anglers on the Bighorn. Because of the density of food in the Bighorn, long, unassuming flats hold high populations of trout. It is often hard to tell where fish are holding in these nondescript areas, unless the trout are feeding on the surface. While fishing these flats is often highly technical, their slow currents provide an efficient area for trout to feed on food that accumulates on the surface and in the surface film. Numerous species, in any number of stages of the emergence, can be found at any one time in these areas. Because of this accumulation of insects on the surface, trout will feed on the flats hours after an emergence or spinner fall has ended. Rising trout on the flats are some of the most formidable adversaries for the match-the-hatch dry-fly angler and are often the most rewarding to bring to net. Don't overlook these flat areas for nymphing either. Nymph rigs with long leaders and light weight fished from the boat will produce trout. Try to find depressions in the bottom, where trout will typically hold. The flats along Red Cliffs, at the bottom of the Landing Strip, and below the Pipeline run are especially effective and fish well year-round.

INSIDE BENDS

These are one of the most efficient areas for trout to feed and are relatively easy places for an angler to present a nymph or dry fly. Inside bends start at the head of a run, often where the current is the fastest; these fast currents push food into the slower current on the inside of the run. Trout that stack up on these inside corners, especially in the uppermost portions, are often the most willing feeders you can find on the river.

These are excellent areas to fish dry flies with a straight upstream approach, especially when fish are feeding in the faster water at the top of the bend. Some of the largest fish feeding to dry flies are found at the head of these pods, gaining access to emerging adults first.

It is important to use extreme caution when approaching an inside bend. Fish can sit in the skinniest of water, just off the main current. These fish are easy to spook. These fish can often be spotted with your eyes and the help of a good pair of polarized sunglasses. I like to make my presentation to these fish from a downstream position. Once you have cast over these fish unsuccessfully—especially with nymphs—they will push out into a less favorable position in the middle of the river seeking shelter. Productive inside bends include One Stop, the Drum Hole, and Crow Beach.

CURRENT EDGES AND SEAMS

These are often extensions of bank feeding lies. Where a bank feature sticks out, a current seam is created a few feet out from the bank. These current seams collect drifting insects, which are easily intercepted by feeding trout. Trout often hold in the calm water between the bank and the seam, moving into the seam to feed. It is important to place your fly in the current seam. If your fly lands in the dead water on the far side of the seam, it will immediately drag. Current seams also occur where two currents come together, typically at the bottom of an island. These areas provide fish with some of the highest concentrations of drifting insects and are easily fished by anglers.

Current edges can be found in just about every river feature on the river and especially around islands, where multiple current edges are available for an angler to fish at one time. Current edges along riffles are one of the best places to find feeding fish on the surface because they both deliver food and offer protection to the trout. Prime examples of current edges and seams can be found at the Split Islands, Three Mile Islands, in No-Name Channel, and throughout the Three Rivers Area.

Anglers fish streamers toward a prime riverbank that offers cover and a current break where fish often hold. JAY NICHOLS

BANKS

Banks are often one of the first places an angler looks to present a fly, especially from the boat, but they are not as important here as they are on many popular freestone rivers. On the Bighorn, fish are focused first on finding efficient food delivery, and many areas provide a better place to consume calories than the bank. I focus my time and my client's time only on banks where bugs collect, either from an eddy or where the current is moving food into the bank at a slow to moderate pace.

While there are several promising cliff walls on the river such as Red Cliffs and Grey Cliffs, most of the riverbanks consist of vegetation that grows to the river's edge. Non-native Russian olive bushes are the dominant vegetation along the river's edge. These bushes hang over the water and trout are often found underneath and along them, especially when large clumps of aquatic grass get caught on them and provide trout with even more protection during the summer.

Overall, the best banks, regardless of their makeup, are the ones where the water depth drops quickly and bugs collect tight to the bank. Deep banks provide protection for fish looking to feed opportunistically on large terrestrials that float by or on other fish that are within striking range of their holding lie. You will always find trout feeding where bugs collect, either in an eddy, along a bank seam, or where the current pushes into the bank.

When I am fishing the banks, I am typically only fishing dry flies or streamers. I don't find that you get a good drift with an indicator rig along the bank, and frankly, there is better water for that type of fishing. If I want to fish a nymph closer to the bank, it is suspended under a dry fly. During high-water periods when the river is above 7,000 cfs, slower bank lies are often good places to target when fishing nymphs toward the bank.

THE MIDDLE

This can consist of a variety of water types including riffles, runs, pools, flats, and tailouts. It's important not to overlook these often nondescript areas in the center of the river. I catch some of my nicest fish with nymphs, streamers, and larger dry flies in the center of the river, especially when river traffic is at its peak.

Trout prefer to sit and feed efficiently in calm areas along the river's edge. But when angling pressure is high on the river, with anglers walking all along the edge and bombarding the banks with cast after cast, fish will find secondary feeding lies in the middle of the river. Fish will also find protection in deeper depths on bright sunny days and during low water.

Midriver tailouts also hold feeding trout in the peak of summer. As water picks up speed in a tailout, right before it flows into the next run, trout feed regularly on the concentration of insects that have accumulated in the flat above. I have taken many nice brown trout over the years in shallow, fast tailouts in the middle of the river. They are certainly worth the time to fish especially with terrestrial patterns.

Angling Pressure and the Trout

The Bighorn River accounts for the third most angler-use days of all the rivers in Montana and is one of the most heavily fished trout fisheries in the country. The result of this angling pressure, and the practice of catch-and-release, significantly impacts the way in which we approach the river and fish for its trout. The cumulative effects of having boats repeatedly floating overhead, anglers wading the river, constantly being presented unnatural offerings, being caught, fighting for their life, and then being released all contribute to a trout's behavior and how they feed.

The unnatural behaviors we introduce into the trout's natural world condition trout to respond in certain ways to our actions. Our artificial actions hone the natural instincts of Bighorn trout, forcing us to continually adapt and to improve our angling techniques in response. For example, a few years ago, when grasshopper fishing was at its all-time best on the Bighorn, fish were continually bombarded with hopper pattern after hopper pattern, often of a similar variety being sold at the shops in Fort Smith. I got in position with my client on a gravel bar 30 feet from a grassy bank, where I had taken many nice brown trout recently. The angler presented one of the river's most natural hopper patterns beautifully, with a reach cast tight along the bank. As the fly drifted, a large brown trout showed itself below the fly and followed it for several feet before rapidly dropping down out of sight. My client presented the fly flawlessly with several other popular Bighorn hopper patterns and the large brown repeated the same response to the fly: rose, followed, and then quickly dropped out of sight.

I dug deep into my box and found a hopper pattern that I had never fished on the Bighorn, yet had worked in western Montana. On the first cast the large brown took the pattern with reckless abandon. While that trout was readily looking to feed on the extreme abundance of grasshoppers located along the banks of the Bighorn that year, it was not going to be fooled by an imitation that it had seen so many times before. This was the trout's conditioned response to the cumulative effect of anglers constantly trying to trick it with the same pattern.

In addition to fly selection, trout develop a conditioned response to many other things that we do as anglers, including fly drag, casting our line over a rising fish, sounds we make when wading, making ourselves visible to the fish when wading, and tendencies that we have when fishing from a boat. The list goes on.

A trout can exhibit behavior derived from a conditioned response throughout the duration of a particular hatch, during the course of a season, or throughout its entire life. This is why large trout can be so hard to catch in any river. An older trout's instincts have been sharpened and honed by the cumulative effect of these conditioned responses to both natural and unnatural behaviors within their environment, making it harder for an angler to catch them.

Trout that have become conditioned by the effects of angling pressure become increasingly more difficult to fool, whether fishing on the surface or below. PAT DORSEY

An angler releases a brown trout back into the Bighorn. JAY NICHOLS

Optimal water conditions and the abundance of food found on the Bighorn make these larger trout slip up more often than on most other rivers. At times it is often complete happenstance that the largest trout on the river are caught. When it happens, it typically occurs from someone nymphing randomly from a boat. Other times it is skill and know-how that bring these large trout to the net by an experienced angler.

Angling pressure should also help dictate how you approach and fish the river. Observe where and how other anglers are fishing. When crowds are at their highest, at the peak of summer, I fish water that others do not, sometimes at different times of the day. I also think about fishing less pressured sections of the river. The Bighorn River offers limitless angling opportunities. Think outside of the box, try new things, and learn to adapt to both the river and the other anglers with whom you share it.

CHAPTER 3

Seasons of the Bighorn

The beauty of a tailwater river, especially one as prolific as the Bighorn, is that anglers can rely on an incredibly high population of trout per mile, fishable river conditions, and an abundance of food that keeps trout feeding routinely. Each season offers anglers its own fishing opportunities and experiences. The timing of the Bighorn fishing seasons differs from those of the calendar year. The overview of the fishing seasons to follow will give you a better understanding of what to expect when choosing a visit for each season. On the Bighorn, you cannot pick a bad time to be on the water.

While the Bighorn is one of the most consistent fisheries during the course of the year, variance in water flows, water temperatures, and weather patterns affect the timing of the insect hatches and the behavior of the fish throughout the seasons. Just because Tricos emerged the last week of July one year doesn't mean that the same is going to happen the next. Snowpack levels in the spring have the most significant impact on the timing of our fishing throughout the year. The amount of snowpack throughout the Bighorn River drainage will impact lake levels each spring. These lake levels will then determine our river flows. Our river flows end up determining the conditions of the river and will directly impact water temperature throughout the season. These water temperatures will have a significant effect on the timing and duration of the hatches.

During high-water years, when flows from the dam exceed 7,500 cfs, water is then released from the top of the dam. This water coming over the top of the dam is significantly warmer than the water that is released from the bottom of the dam. As we saw in 2011, when flows reached 13,000 cfs, the water warmed up quickly and some of our best dry-fly fishing occurred in June. Yellow Sally and Pale Morning Dun emergences were prolific and people were amazed at how good the fishing was in flows four to five times higher than normal. These hatches came off with greater intensity, but were also shorter because of the rapid increase in water temperature.

The Bighorn River can be an outstanding trout fishery 365 days a year. Understanding how the river changes with the seasons will help you determine when you want to fish the Bighorn. JAY NICHOLS

Conversely, 2012 was a low-water year and the best insect emergences occurred in August. During years when the river only sees bottom-release flows, reaching water temperatures conducive to good insect emergences takes significantly longer. In addition to temperature, low-water years, especially in consecutive years like we most recently saw from 2002–2008, cause increased sedimentation in the river. This increased sedimentation can impact the diversity, intensity, and duration of the insect hatches that we see in any given year.

Spring

Spring is a magical time on the Bighorn. Not only is it the start of another angling season full of optimism and promise, but it is also an awakening for the river. The reservoir is filled by snowmelt, water temperatures begin to climb, trout metabolism rises, birds migrate, trees bud, insect emergences become more frequent, and, most importantly, the placid surface of the river is dimpled once again by rising trout.

Fishing the Flows

The Bighorn River during any given year can range from 1,500 cubic feet per second (cfs) to 12,000-plus cfs. Ideal flows for anglers typically range from 2,000 cfs to 4,500 cfs throughout the year. These varying outflows are a result of snowpack levels in the mountains and rainfall that occurs within a massive geographic area of Montana and Wyoming. This vast area of Wyoming includes both the Wind and Bighorn Mountain ranges, along with the Wind, Shoshone, and Bighorn Rivers. The amount of water being released from the dam is important to Bighorn River fly fishers for several reasons. The flow of the river affects where trout will lie in the river and what insects they have to feed on, and it often dictates what techniques anglers can use to catch them.

Anglers planning a trip should be familiar with how inflows from snowpack levels and rainfall affect reservoir levels and how dam managers manipulate outflows based on current inflow and reservoir levels. Thanks to the Internet, you get instantaneous data for inflows, outflows, snowpack levels, and reservoir levels: www.usbr.gov/gp-bin/arcweb_bhr.pl

High-water years occur on the Bighorn when snowpack levels are significantly higher than average and spring rainfall is high. During these years the reservoir reaches 100 percent capacity and inflows significantly exceed outflows. To make room for the resulting inflows, dam managers need to increase the outflow of water into the river to reduce reservoir levels. These increased outflows results in a "spring runoff effect" that occurs naturally each year on freestone rivers. Once inflows decrease into the reservoir, the outflows will correspond accordingly. This spring runoff effect doesn't occur most years. During the worst high-water years, runoff will last for six to eight weeks and flows can peak as high as 15,000 cfs, yet the river will remain fishable the whole time.

During low-water years, spring runoff simply does not occur because there isn't enough snowpack and/or rainfall to fill the reservoir; therefore, there is no need for managers to increase outflows. During low-water years, river levels rarely change throughout the entire year. An ideal year would consist of flows that average around 2,500 cfs throughout the year, with dam managers increasing flows in the spring for a short two- to four-day period that is necessary for reducing sedimentation in the river. This short "flush" would promote a healthy river system by flushing sediment and debris downriver. On most low-water years, we rarely see flows that average 2,500 cfs, and there is simply not enough water for dam managers to initiate a flush. Even with the incredibly large reservoir that supports the Bighorn River, water-use priorities and Mother Nature often dictate Bighorn River flows from year to year. Each flow level in the Bighorn River will create a unique set of river conditions that dictate how trout will behave. These changing conditions will also dictate the techniques an angler should use to be successful.

1,750–4,500 cfs. These flows are what most anglers should expect when fishing the Bighorn. I would consider this range to be the base flows throughout the year. During low-water years, expect flows to average at or below 2,000 cfs, and during an average year to find around 3,000 cfs. Throughout this flow range the Bighorn is at its most enjoyable to fish. Anglers are able to both float and wade the river with ease and comfort with flows at or above 2,500 cfs, including the river's numerous side channels. Also, every technique, including dry flies, nymphs, and streamers, works well, and the fish hold throughout the entire river channel.

4,500–7,500 cfs. At these river flows, the river is typically in transition and either on the way up or down, as runoff is occurring or tapering off. We typically see flows in this range during May and June and possibly into early July during extreme high-water years. During this flow stage, nymph fishing is typically best, but you can still have dry-fly opportunities. The one thing we typically don't like to see is large, quick jumps in the water during this time. Small, calculated bumps, if you will, are best for the fishing. The river at this flow stage is still wadable, becoming more challenging as it reaches the 7,000 cfs mark. You can wade around islands, in side channels, or by well-defined inside bends. The fishing is still good at this time.

7,500–12,000+ cfs. These are the largest flows we see on the river and only occur during high-water years, typically in late May or June. At these flows, nymph fishing from the boat is your best bet and often your only option. Rowing the river once flows reach 7,000 cfs or higher can be a serious hazard for novice oarsmen. It is a much better idea to hire an experienced guide. Nymph fishing from the boat will remain consistent with long leaders, extra weight, and double nymph rigs.

Wade fishing for the most part is out of the question until the water gets so high that it goes over the river's banks, which typically occurs at 10,500 cfs or higher. I have had excellent dry-fly fishing at this time when trout are feeding in areas that used to be dry grass. It is amazing to see how quickly trout will adapt to their food sources at this time. Another thing to keep in mind is that once the water releases exceed 7,500 cfs, water begins to flow over the top of Yellowtail Dam rather than only from the bottom. This brings the water temperature up in the river, which jump starts our summer hatches of PMDs and Yellow Sallies and triggers the growth of aquatic vegetation in the river. ■

For locals and regional residents, spring is often their favorite time to be on the river. While the weather can be volatile, spring offers some of the most consistent and reliable fishing. Early spring is an overlooked time of the year on the Bighorn, and all of Montana for that matter, especially by traveling anglers. DAVID PALMER

The spring season runs from March through May. Average daily high temperatures range from the mid- to upper 40s Fahrenheit in March to the lower 70s in May and April and can feature just about anything in between. Rain and snow can be expected at any time, especially in March and April. Typically, expect the mornings to be cold in the upper 30s or low 40s, with temperatures warming up quickly in the late morning. Water temperatures will range from 36 to 50 degrees, and are most often in the low to mid-40s.

The first mayfly hatches of the year start on the lower river, below Bighorn Access down to Two Leggins Access. Water temperatures in the lower 40s are conducive to excellent hatches of midges and Blue-Winged Olives and a high rate of activity by the trout. Because of its distance from the dam, the lower river can reach these ideal temperatures two to three weeks before the upper river. These first hatches of mayflies won't be as intense or as widespread as on the upper river, but they do offer great opportunity for dry-fly fishing. When fishing the lower river at this time, I like to rig two rods—one for streamers and one for dry flies. As I float this stretch, I often fish streamers in between pods of rising trout.

While hatches often start earlier on the lower river, the upper river offers a far greater abundance of insects. In addition to the dependable Blue-Winged Olives, incredible emergences of midges occur as well. Trout also feed freely on scuds and sow bugs. Because of this abundance of food, most anglers focus their time each spring on the upper thirteen miles of the river. Coinciding with increased insect activity is an increase in the trout's metabolism, and the trout feed actively daily, both on the surface and underneath.

Holding water in spring is also easier to read on the upper river. Once water temperatures increase and daily hatch activity occurs, trout will begin to move from their slow, deep winter lies to more active feeding stations. With water temperatures still relatively cold, you will typically find fish feeding just off of the main current. Expect fish to be more concentrated at this time. Once you find fish in a particular spot, there will be many in that spot. Fish that water and other water like it thoroughly. During the spring, you will find fish sitting in moderately paced water along current edges and seams.

Midges (#16-22) can hatch at any time of the day, and the timing and duration of these hatches are dependent on weather and water temperature. You will typically find hatching midges in the late morning or early afternoon during the warmest part of the day, as well as during late afternoon and early evening. Some of the best surface fishing with midges occurs when the adult midges cluster in the early afternoon and the evening.

Midge larval and pupal patterns work well through the spring, with black, cream, root beer, red, and olive being the best colors. Fish your larva and pupa imitations in slower runs until you begin to see noses and snouts popping up for the duns or head-and-tail rises to the emergers. Fish eating midges tend to pod up. The key to success on the top is locating these feeding groups of fish. Prospect the prime water with subsurface imitations until the feeding frenzy begins on top. Once fish begin feeding on top, look for clustering to occur as these midges begin to mate. Trout key in on these clusters routinely. Amazingly enough, one of the best midge emergences I have ever seen was on a bright sunny day when air temperatures reached 103 degrees. The water was colder than average for the month of May and an early season heat wave moved into southeast Montana; the water warmed up a few degrees and was just enough to create a massive hatch.

Blue-Winged Olives (BWOs) are the main event in the spring, and the trout feed with fervor, both on the surface and below, when these size 16 to 20 mayflies are present. The BWO hatch is the first significant insect

The weather during the spring may not always be reliable as the fishing is. Here guide Bryen Venema hooks up during a spring midge emergence. Overcast skies and no wind are often the perfect recipe for abundant midge and Blue-Winged Olive emergences. DAVID PALMER

hatch after winter, and provides the trout with a large total amount of food. They respond accordingly. If you haven't experienced a BWO hatch on the Horn, you have been missing out. The magic water temperature that seems to trigger spring Blue-Winged Olive emergences is right around 43 degrees. Once this hatch begins, trout gorge on every stage of the hatch: nymphs, emergers, duns, and spinners are all important. Nymph fishing during this hatch can be just as good, if not better, than the action on top.

The BWO hatch, during a typical day, can last anywhere from one hour to six, depending on its intensity. It typically starts around midday or early afternoon and can last until dark. It can start as early as late March and continue well into the summer, with the peak being from the end of April until the third week of May. In the low-water year of 2013, the BWO hatch continued, without interruption, well into the summer. In spring it is possible to fish a morning midge hatch, an afternoon BWO hatch, and both BWO and midge patterns in the early evening. On some days, dry-fly fishing is superb from the time you hit the water to the time you leave.

Peak angler traffic during the spring season coincides with the Blue-Winged Olive hatch and is often during the last two weeks of April and the first two weeks of May. Late March and early April is a great time of year to take advantage of spring fishing opportunities without the crowds. Anglers looking to fish the peak spring window should find guides and accommodations in Fort Smith well in advance. The spring peak window, like the other seasonal peak windows, fills up quickly, often a year in advance.

While most anglers fish nymphs and dry flies imitating the prominent midge and Blue-Winged Olive emergences, streamers fished deep and slow will consistently catch fish throughout the entire river. The lower river is especially good for covering water with a streamer imitation.

Unlike freestone streams, there is no spring runoff on the upper Bighorn. The Bighorn experiences an "artificial" runoff that only occurs when snowfall amounts throughout the region are high and/or significant rainfall occurs in the spring. Increased flows occur when the reservoir reaches full pool and inflows are higher than outflows as dam managers increase flows into the river to evacuate water from the lake, but the water remains clear.

On one occasion I saw the upper 3 miles of the river off-color. This occurred for one day after a rainstorm that dumped almost 6 inches of rain in 48 hours. On that day, I was one of the only guides on the river, and it still fished well, even while off-color. Average water flows in spring are typically around 2,000 to 3,000 cfs. During the worst of runoff years, when reservoir levels reach flood stage, water releases from the dam can reach 10,000 to 15,000 cfs. While these flows are simply huge, they don't happen often and, amazingly, the river still fishes well even at these high flows.

Nymph fishermen can find great success during the spring season. Bighorn trout gorge on midge pupae and small mayfly nymphs throughout the day. PAT DORSEY

During spring runoff, lower river tributaries such as Rotten Grass Creek (above) can turn the river brown and make fishing a challenge until they run clear.

When high-water years occur, increased water releases from the dam typically start in May and last until mid-June or early July. During runoff, the upper 10 miles of the river remain clear and fishable, regardless of water releases from the dam. The first major tributary that can turn the water off-color is Soap Creek, about 10 river miles from the dam. The effects of dirty water being carried into the river by Soap Creek and other tributaries, such as Rotten Grass, Mountain Pocket, and Hay Coulee Creeks, make the lower river below Bighorn Fishing Access often unfishable. With that being said, these tributaries tend to clear relatively quickly. Check with local fly shops to find out about current runoff conditions throughout the river.

Spring Fly Box

Nymphs
Zebra Midge (#18-22; red, black, cream, olive)
Yong Midge (#18-20; brown, cream)
Red Midge Larva (#12-20)
Root Beer Midge (#18-20)
Quill Nymph (#18-20; black, olive)
Wonder Nymph (#18-20; black, olive)
Ray Charles (#14-18; gray, pink, tan)
Firebead Sow Bug (#14-18; pink, tan)
Berg's Scud (#14-16; pink, orange)

Dry Flies
Parachute Adams (#16-22; gray, olive)
Sipper Emerger (#18-20; gray, olive)
CDC Transitional Midge (#18-20, gray)
Crippled Thor (#18-20, olive)
Griffith's Gnat (#18-22)
Twilight Paramidge (#18-20)
Student Emerger (#18-20, gray)
CDC Sparkle Dun (#18-20; gray, olive)

Streamers
Sparkle Minnow (#4-6, sculpin)
Peanut Envy (#4-6; olive, black, white)
Bonefish Clouser (#6-10)
Woolly Bugger (#4-10; black, olive, tan)
JR's Conehead Streamer (#6; olive, black, tan)

Summer

Endless days, prolific hatches, and an abundance of ideal trout water make summer fishing on the Bighorn hard to beat. During summer the trout's metabolism is at its peak, conditions are right for copious hatches, and the trout actively feed throughout the day. During the course of the day, the trout's activity and feeding rhythm coincide with the river's numerous summer insect hatches. Trout key in on hatches of Pale Morning Duns, Yellow Sallies, Black Caddis, Tan Caddis, Tricos, and *Baetis* throughout the summer and continue feeding on the abundance of crustaceans subsurface.

Anglers who prefer to fish dry flies will find plenty of opportunity. Any of the insect hatches mentioned above can be present at any given time, often overlapping. A quick stop in a fly shop will give you a general idea of what to expect, but anglers should be prepared for anything. The Black Caddis hatch is the crown jewel of summer dry-fly fishing. This river-wide hatch lingers for a long time, and starts at the end of July some years and lasts into September. Two species of Black Caddis come off in the afternoon and evenings—the first is a larger size 16, and the other is size 18 to 20.

Anglers can also experience excellent match-the-hatch dry-fly fishing with Tan Caddis, Pale Morning Duns, Yellow Sallies, and Tricos. The appearance, timing, and duration of these hatches vary greatly from year

Seemingly endless Montana summer days provide anglers with great fishing from June through mid-September. Average daily air temperatures reach the 80s and 90s during the warmest part of the day, with nighttime lows in the 50s. With average temperatures in September around 75, you can expect summer fishing conditions to exist into mid-September. Water temperatures are in the mid-50s to low 60s, depending on the section of the river and the relationship to the dam. HALE HARRIS

Ashley Garrison found this rainbow tailing in a small side channel riffle. The fish took a floating Pale Morning Dun nymph fished in the surface film.

to year, as does the section of the river that they show up on. In 2012, for example, intense hatches of Tricos and Tan Caddis emerged on the upper river during all of August. Anglers who showed up in 2013 expected the same experience as they had in 2012, but because 2013 was a low-water year with cold water temperatures, Tricos and Tan Caddis did not appear on the upper river during August.

However, Tricos were emerging daily on the lower river where water temperatures were warmer, particularly from Mallard's to Two Leggins, and most anglers who had experienced the great fishing on the upper river in 2012 were unaware or unwilling to venture down to the lower river at that time. The Tricos eventually did end up emerging on the upper river in 2013 but, because of cold water temperatures, not until October. The same was true of the Tan Caddis emergence. Just when we thought they weren't going to emerge at all on the upper river in 2013, they showed up in October.

In addition to these aquatic insects, terrestrial insects such as grasshoppers, ants, and beetles bring trout to the surface readily. The intensity of the hopper hatch tends to be cyclic from one year to the next. It seems like the grasshopper fishing is often the best when the aquatic insect hatches are not. The lack of aquatic insects forces fish to expend more energy in pursuit of these larger terrestrial meals. Some of the largest brown trout are caught during the first week of hopper fishing each year.

Terrestrial fishing can be great river-wide, but it really brings the lower river to life. There is nothing better than getting that toilet-bowl-flush eat from a large trout as your fly drifts over likely holding water. When terrestrial fishing, I often use a dry-dropper setup, and if the trout seem to favor the dry, I will fish double dry flies or fish one larger dry with movement. Otherwise, I leave the nymph on 20 to 24 inches below the dry. This is an effective way to prospect the shallow water holding lies where trout often feed at this time of the year.

While dry-fly fishing is the main attraction of summer, below the surface there is also an abundance of scuds, sow bugs, midges, mayfly nymphs, caddis pupae, and aquatic worms available to the trout, and nymph fishing is also incredibly consistent. While using a long line indicator nymph rig is effective from the boat, using a spring creek nymph rig to fish the skinny water or sight-nymph is an exciting way to fish. These shorter rigs are also better for cutting through the floating moss that is often present at this time of the year.

This is also a great time to swing soft-hackles to imitate emerging insects in the riffles, which is an often overlooked technique. The anglers that enjoy doing it have great success. The beauty of swinging soft-hackles is that you can do it on a dry line, often more enjoyable than a heavy indicator nymph rig.

In general, when nymph fishing in summer, if an insect is emerging, you should assume the trout are taking that food source selectively. When

Surrounded by agricultural fields along its length, terrestrial fishing on the Bighorn can be fantastic. Here Bighorn Angler co-owner Pete Shanafelt shows off a brown trout that ate a Morrish Hopper. JAY NICHOLS

insects are not visibly emerging, fishing sow bugs, or other impressionistic patterns, will take opportunistically feeding fish throughout the day.

Streamers are typically not the preferred choice of anglers in the summer. However, those dedicated to streamer fishing year-round should fish smaller patterns in more neutral colors. I would fish them on a floating line and cover shallower water. I have definitely had some banner summer season streamer days. Anglers searching out large fish can fish an unconventional dry-dropper rig that consists of a large hopper with a leech pattern fished underneath. This rig is not for everyone, but it does result in some quality trout.

Because of water temperatures that can reach the mid-60s and an abundance of insect activity, trout move into faster water and riffles. Besides providing trout with an efficient place to feed on caddis and mayflies, these fast-water lies provide increased oxygen to the fish as well. The warmer the water, the more likely you are to find fish in these spots. Many of these riffles that the fish move into are shallow. As an angler, be sure to fish the skinniest of water. This kind of fishing takes practice. Catching trout routinely in less than a foot of water is an exercise in seeing

During the summer Bighorn trout move into the well-oxygenated riffle water to feed. Here guide Seth Byler takes advantage of these concentrated trout. JAY NICHOLS

Aquatic vegetation is a natural part of any tailwater river. While at times it can be a nuisance to anglers, especially to nymph fishermen, at other times it adds a welcome dynamic. Here an angler works an area of the Bighorn that better resembles a spring creek.

is believing. I can't stress enough how important these areas are in the dog days of summer. Approach these shallow riffles cautiously. Often, when aquatic vegetation grows in these shallow riffles, brown trout will stand out against the green backdrop. Sight-nymphing to these fish is a blast. A dry-dropper rig or spring creek nymph setup works well for this also.

Aquatic vegetation can be found in the Bighorn year-round; however, in early August, warmer water temperatures combined with the river's nutrient-rich water promote the abundant growth of aquatic vegetation, which grows in the slower water first and slowly works its way up along the edges of the faster water. This aquatic vegetation fills in the river channel, pushing the river's water up and out and slowing the overall speed of the river.

At this time, anglers who nymph should focus on gravel areas in the riffles and along the banks and faster water channels cut amongst the weeds in the middle of the river. Trout will also use the current breaks created by surface vegetation as prime feeding lies to intercept insects on the surface. Try to find ways to use this aquatic vegetation to your advantage. It often concentrates trout.

The abundant aquatic grass is cyclic, growing in the warmer months, then dying and breaking free once water temperatures drop, typically in late October. Anglers won't find it to be a nuisance until it begins to drift throughout the water column. While this broken vegetation can impede an

Summer Fly Box

Nymphs
Tungsten Split Case PMD (#14-18)
Quill Nymph (#18-20; black, cream)
Soft-Hackle Ray Charles (#14-20; gray, pink, tan)
San Juan Worm (#6-12; red, red/brown, wine)
Poodle Sniffer (#16-18)
Pheasant Tail (#16-22; olive, brown)
Killer Bug (#14-18; pink, gray)
Split Case PMD (#16-20)
Soft-Hackle Sow Bug (#16-20; pink, tan)

Dry Flies
CDC Black Caddis (#16-20)
CDC Sparkle Dun (#14-22; gray, olive)
Translucent Emerger (#14-16; brown, tan)
Bloom's Flying Ant (#12-16; black, cinnamon)
Panty Dropper Hopper (#8-12, tan)
Paraspinner (#14-22; rusty, olive)
Trico Spinner (#18-22)
The Student (#18-22, gray)

Streamers
Delektable Screamer (#4, black/olive)
Meat Whistle (#2-6; brown, black)
Bonefish Clouser (#4-8)

angler's ability to present a fly at times, great fishing can still be had by adjusting your technique and by being diligent about dealing with it.

As any guide will tell you, if there is moss on your fly, you will catch nothing. Anglers need to get their flies down quickly to the bottom and pick them up out of the water quickly to recast to keep their flies free of moss. Shorter leaders and heavier weight definitely help. Letting your indicator nymph rig swing below you downstream is a sure-fire way of collecting weeds.

Anglers should check their flies after every cast and use the "Bighorn Smack" technique to keep their flies clean. This technique is achieved by keeping your rod tip high and moving your arm in large circles, smacking only your flies against the surface of the water. This is an effective and efficient way of clearing your nymph rig of moss.

Fall

The Bighorn Valley is a special place come fall. The riverside cottonwoods set the river's edge ablaze with vivid oranges, yellows, and reds. Rooster pheasants cackle in nearby fields and the river's brown trout are dressed in vibrant spawning colors. The fishing on the Bighorn comes full circle with the arrival of the fall season, which lasts from mid-September through November.

While the autumn solstice occurs at the end of September, summer-like weather often continues throughout the month. Because of the high desert geography of eastern Montana, the climate of the Bighorn Valley is much more temperate than the rest of the state in the fall. It also takes much longer for water temperatures to cool because of the massive

A perfect autumn day brings the author's father incredible dry-fly fishing. Here Vince Galletta casts to rising fish during a Trico emergence on a dead calm, full overcast day.

volume of water stored in Bighorn Lake. This warm water coming from Bighorn Lake creates ideal fall fishing conditions on the Bighorn, promoting prolific insect hatches and trout activity.

A few smaller-sized mayfly hatches and streamer fishing dominate the fishing this time of year. The summer dry-fly fishing often carries over into fall on the Bighorn. The prominent Trico dun emergences and spinner falls normally last well into October. On cooler mornings the dun emergences are the best, while the spinner falls require warm, sunny days.

In addition to the Trico hatch, there is another small mayfly emergence, the *Pseudocloeon*. These size 20 to 24 Blue-Winged Olives hatch in droves on calm, cloudy days. Anglers should approach this hatch the same way they would fish any other Blue-Winged Olive emergence. Fine tippets down to 6X, sparse patterns, and precise presentation are required mainly because of their small size. Some anglers find fishing the *Pseudocloeon* hatch to be too frustrating, while others enjoy the challenge of catching a big fish on a small fly. By late October, or once cooler weather arrives, larger fall *Baetis* enter the mix and hatch well into

Bighorn Angler guide Seth Byler displays the bounty of the fall season. Brown trout become increasingly aggressive during the fall season and charge well-presented streamers. I typically fish an intermediate sink tip in the fall. These tips allow you to fish the whole river effectively—along the banks and in the middle. JAY NICHOLS

November, though they are not nearly as prolific as the spring hatches. While Pseudos fish the best in the upper river, I find the larger fall Blue-Winged Olive hatch to fish well on the lower river.

Once colder fall nights move into the area, the river begins to cool and brown trout preparing for their fall spawn become aggressive and highly susceptible to a well-presented streamer pattern. With ideal water temperatures, both the upper and lower river fish well. Covering long stretches of the river from a drift boat is the best way to efficiently fish streamers during the fall. Excellent streamer fishing is usually had throughout the season and into December.

The biggest factor affecting fishing conditions is the "turnover" of Bighorn Lake (see page 9) when algae, moss, and other plant matter on the surface of the lake sink and are sent into the river through the bottom releases of Yellowtail Dam. The severity of this turnover differs from year to year but it usually occurs sometime in October. In most cases, it only turns the river off-color and deposits "gunk" into the river for a short period, which only affects the first few miles of the river. In more severe years, the river can turn to pea soup and wreak havoc on anglers for an extended period of time. It is hard to predict when this will occur, but cold days combined with cold evenings are a good indication that it is near. The lake turnover affects nymph fishing the most, if and when it occurs. During normal years, nymph fishing remains good throughout the fall, as rainbows transition to winter lies and browns prepare for the spawn.

The brown trout spawn routinely occurs later on the Bighorn than on just about any other river in Montana. It most often occurs in November and can last into December. As with the spring rainbow spawn, the timing and duration depends on water temperatures, with the ideal spawning range being in the low 50s. Once these browns finish their spawn, they will leave the spawning beds and move into slower water for the winter.

With average air temperatures in the 60s throughout October, it is one of my favorite months to fish the river. Most of September sees moderate to heavy fishing pressure, but by early October traffic is relatively light on the river. Visiting anglers continue to fish into November, with the last push coinciding with the Thanksgiving holiday weekend.

Anglers should be prepared to see all four seasons of weather and a variety of potential water conditions during a fall trip to the Bighorn. Ideally, we hope for the conditions shown above. JAY NICHOLS

Fall Fly Box

Nymphs
Tungteaser (#18-20, black)
Pheasant Tail (#18-22; olive, brown)
Ray Charles (#16-20; pink, gray, tan)
Killer Bug (#16-18, pink)
Pseudo Wonder Nymph (#20-22)
San Juan Worm (#6-12; red, brown, wine, red/brown)

Dry Flies
The Student (#18-22, gray)
Parachute Adams (#18-22; gray, olive, cream)
Rusty Spinner (#16-22; rusty, olive)
CDC Sparkle Dun (#18-22; gray, olive)
Trico Paraspinner (#18-22)

Streamers
Woolly Bugger (#2-10; black, olive, tan)
Slumpbuster (#4-8; black, olive)
Bonefish Clouser (#4-8)
Sparkle Minnow (#2-6, sculpin)
Circus Peanut (#4-6; black, olive, yellow)
JR's Conehead Streamer (#4-6; olive, white, tan)
Lil Kim (#4-8, copper)
Delektable Screamer (#4, olive/black)
Bighorn Bugger (#4-8, yellow/brown)

Winter

By the time winter arrives, the river has been left mostly to the migratory ducks and geese that use the Bighorn River as a major flyway in their southern migration and hunters that brave below-freezing temperatures to shoot a limit of birds.

The river is most often frequented by local anglers who take advantage of pleasant weather windows. Sun-filled days are surprisingly comfortable and produce good fishing. December and January see the least amount of fishing pressure, with average temperatures more conducive to tying flies and preparing for the next season.

Dam managers will typically set a winter flow for the river in the fall based on current reservoir levels and maintain that flow, for the most part, until spring. By the time the New Year has arrived, nearly all of the river's aquatic vegetation has broken up and been flushed down river. This, combined with near-constant water temperatures that keep the river predominately ice-free, produces good nymph fishing when the weather cooperates.

Midge larvae and pupae, along with scuds and sow bugs, are standard winter fare and vital to the trout's health. This winter forage base, common in tailwater fisheries, gives trout the ability to feed and remain healthy all year. With the trout's metabolism at its lowest point, trout lurk up in the slowest holding lies. When fishing the best winter water, at times

Winter offers anglers peace and tranquility and some really good nymph fishing on warmer days. Most anglers focus their time on the upper 3 miles of the river during the winter.
HALE HARRIS

Anglers willing to brave the elements still find success even during the worst weather conditions. HALE HARRIS

it may seem as if your strike indicator is barely moving downstream, if at all. All of a sudden your indicator will twitch, and a trout will be on.

Streamer fishing can also be good and flies fished methodically throughout the river, on sinking lines, will bring the most success. The lower river can fish well as water temperatures will run warmer than the upper river near the dam.

Once we move into February and we start to experience a few breaks from winter's icy grip, sporadic midge emergences will begin to occur on warm, sunny afternoons. Anglers should be on the river during the warmest part of the day to take advantage of this first chance of the year to fish dry flies.

Winter Fly Box

Nymph
Tungteaser (#18-20, black)
Ray Charles (#16-20; gray, pink, tan)
Firebead Sow Bug (#14-18; pink, tan)
Pheasant Tail (#18-20; olive, brown)
Zebra Midge (#18-20; red, black)
Bighorn Scud (#14-16; orange, pink)
Quill Nymph (#18-20; black, olive)

Dry Flies
The Student (#18-22, gray)
Parachute Adams (#18-22; gray, olive)
Student Emerger (#18-20, gray)

Streamers
Bonefish Clouser (#4-8)
Slumpbuster (#4-8; black, olive)
Sparkle Minnow (#4-6, sculpin)

CHAPTER 4

River Stretches

From Afterbay Dam in Fort Smith, Montana, the Bighorn River offers anglers 35 miles of trout water as it meanders it way north to the town of Hardin. The Bighorn River is typically broken down into two larger segments—the upper and lower river. The upper river is considered the first 13 miles of the river, from Afterbay Access to Bighorn Access, and is what most people are referring to when they mention the famous tailwater. While this 13-mile stretch of river is quite possibly the best stretch of any trout river in the world, it is not the only good trout water on the Bighorn River. Veteran anglers and guides alike know that the lower river from Bighorn Access to Two Leggins also offers tremendous trout-fishing opportunity.

Throughout this entire stretch of blue-ribbon trout water, the Bighorn River offers an abundance of access to both wade anglers and float fly fishers alike. While contained within the confines of the Crow Indian Reservation, designated access to the river is granted in trust to the public by the state of Montana and the federal government of the United States.

The National Park Service and Montana FWP provide five well-developed access points with permanent boat ramps and wading access. To access the river via these sites, a Montana fishing license is required. At the two uppermost accesses, Afterbay Access and Three Mile Access, a $5.00 per day or $30.00 annual parking pass is required. Anyone who is at least 62 years old can purchase a Lifetime Senior National Park Pass for a one-time fee of $10. This Senior Pass allows access to all national parks and a permanent pass to the Bighorn accesses; it needs to be displayed in your vehicle each day you use Afterbay or Three Mile sites. Parking passes can be purchased manually at the National Park visitor's center, which is located on the Fort Smith side of the river, right before Afterbay Dam. Senior national park passes can be purchased at the national park headquarters located three miles south of Fort Smith on Highway 313. Once in the river, state law comes into effect, and you are able to move legally from bank to bank, within the river's high-water mark.

Overview

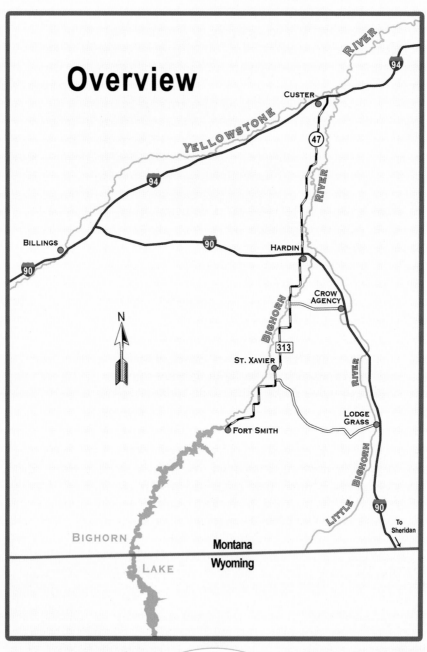

Having this state waterway encapsulated by the Crow Reservation has protected the river from the development seen on many of the other famous trout fisheries throughout Montana. Riverfront development is extremely limited, and much of the tribal land the river flows through is as wild as ever, which provides anglers with an ideal setting for a day on the river.

While rarely used by anglers because of the abundance of access via federal and state access points, other limited access to the river is possible through the Crow Reservation. If you would like access to Crow tribal lands for fishing or hunting purposes, permits can be purchased via the tribe in the town of Crow Agency, Montana. If you are not within the confines of an official state or federal access point, or within the high-water mark on the river, you are on either Crow or private land. By accessing the river at a well-marked site, you will ensure that you are within compliance and can move freely once in the river.

Thanks to moderate flows and a uniform streambed, the Bighorn River is ideal for anglers of all ages and abilities to both wade and float fish. Good wade fishing can be had at all of the federal and state fishing access sites on the river. Anglers can easily move within the high-water mark both up- and downriver from these sites. Because of the size of the river, there are not many places to cross. It is possible in a few spots for experienced waders to cross the river when flows are less than 2,000 cubic feet per second. For anglers looking to gain access to the other side of the

Guide Bob Bergquist launches his boat at the well-maintained Afterbay boat ramp.

river and water in between these access points, they should use some form of watercraft.

With few obstacles and, for the most part, a wide, slow-moving flow throughout its length, the Bighorn River is one of the easiest rivers in Montana to float. With relatively few accesses and numerous river miles between each, floating the Bighorn is the most efficient way to fish the river. While floating in a drift boat allows anglers to effectively fish water they would not be able to access otherwise, many people use their boat as a taxi—taking them from wade spot to wade spot. By getting out of the boat, anglers can concentrate their efforts on the best areas of the river.

While the various stretches of the Bighorn River are relatively easy to navigate by boat, there are a few hazards oarsmen need to be aware of. The first is the Suck Hole, located river right, just about a mile below Afterbay Dam. The other is the Two Leggins diversion dam located a half mile above the Two Leggins Fishing Access. If floating the river for the first time, you should inquire locally about these possible hazards.

Drift boats are the most popular watercraft used to float the Bighorn River. Anglers looking to access the many miles of trout filled water between each access point also use pontoon boats, water masters, and kayaks. For anglers with a good grasp on fishing the Bighorn, renting a drift boat is a good option. Several operations in Fort Smith rent drift boats at a reasonable price. It is wise to have some basic understanding of rowing a boat before renting one. This will keep you from causing trouble for both yourself and other river users. Conflicts that occur on the river because of inexperienced oarsmen are one of the most frequent complaints you will

The Bighorn offers anglers 35 miles of prime wade and float fishing opportunity as the river flows north between the towns of Fort Smith and Hardin, Montana. PAUL RUHTER

The Bighorn is one of the easiest rivers to navigate by boat or foot in the West, making it a great river for anglers of all ages and abilities. JAY NICHOLS

hear about from other anglers. Having a pod of fish you are fishing be run over or, worse yet, you or your boat being run into by an inexperienced oarsman, is never a positive experience. If you are not able to navigate a boat properly, it's best to hire a guide or wade fish.

The Upper River

Anglers from around the world come to fish the 13-mile stretch of river from Afterbay to Bighorn Access. I would make an educated guess that this portion accounts for almost 90 percent of angler-use days on the Bighorn, and for good reason. This stretch is the most stable, has the highest trout populations and the most consistent hatches, and is the closest to Fort Smith.

This stretch has three main access points. Afterbay Access is the first and offers a large parking lot and ample space to launch a boat on the west side of the river. Afterbay boat launch can be chaotic in the mornings during peak times. Quickly launch your boat so others can do the same.

Please do not ready your boat on or while blocking the boat ramp. It is best to do so in the staging area. While not officially marked, there is federal land on the Fort Smith (east) side of the river, across from Afterbay Dam, that offers wade access as well. While there is no camping at Afterbay Access, a few miles up on either side of the Afterbay Reservoir there are well-maintained federal campsites.

Three miles downstream from Afterbay Access is Three Mile Access, which also offers a paved boat ramp and ample foot access to the river. This access is the most widely used by wade anglers. Upstream from the Three Mile Access there is a 1.3-mile trail maintained by the federal government. This stretch of river was first settled by the Lind family and later purchased by the federal government. You may still hear some people refer to this access as the Lind Access.

The last access on the upper 13 is Bighorn Access, located 13 miles from Afterbay Access and 10 miles from Three Mile Access. This is the most popular take-out, because floaters putting in at Afterbay and Three Mile use this site. This access has two nicely paved boat ramps, primitive campsites, and vaulted toilets maintained by Montana FWP. Thirteen Mile Access, also called Thirteen Mile, offers anglers a nice place to set up camp along the river at the end of the day.

Here anglers float through the Drum Hole, a prime run on the first three miles of the upper river. HALE HARRIS

Three main floats are available to anglers on these upper 13 river miles—Afterbay to Three Mile Access, Three Mile to Bighorn Access, and Afterbay to Bighorn. All three of these floats are popular among anglers, depending on how many river miles they are looking to float and fish each day.

The Upper 13 is a bug factory with excellent populations of aquatic insects, including mayflies such as Blue-Winged Olives, Pale Morning Duns, and Tricos, as well as midges, Black and Tan Caddis, and Yellow Sallies. In addition to the high density of aquatic insects, what really sets this upper section of the river apart is the astounding density of crustaceans. Scuds and sow bugs thrive on the clean, gravel bottom covered in aquatic vegetation. Sow bug imitations are effective every day of the year on the upper river. The year-round availability of sow bugs and scuds, along with the seasonal appearance of aquatic insects, are the primary reasons trout in this section are so abundant and grow so quickly.

Trout populations in this 13-mile stretch of river during some years are as high as 7,500 trout per mile, with around 5,000 trout per mile during a normal year. The farther you move from the dam, the slightly lower the trout per mile counts become, but the fishing continues to be excellent all the way to Bighorn Access.

AFTERBAY TO THREE MILE
Afterbay to Three Mile (referred to as the Upper 3) is one of the most popular stretches of trout water in Montana, if not the world. If someone were trying to artificially create a world-class fishery for the enjoyment of a fly angler, this would be it. Clear water flows over fine gravel and aquatic vegetation through trout-filled riffles, runs, flats, and shelves that hold trout every inch of the way. The Upper 3 produces tremendous opportunity to catch fish every day of the year and offers the largest trout populations per mile on the river (5,000 to 7,000 per mile).

The Upper 3 is the most widely used section of river by wade anglers. Walking anglers can find abundant wade access downriver from Afterbay Access and upriver from Three Mile Access. A trail at Afterbay Access offers several miles of walk-in access to the long straight run below Afterbay Dam, along with the water around First Island and the Meat Hole. At First Island, the river picks up speed for the first time, after the quarter-mile flat below the dam, and at the bottom of First Island is the Meat Hole, a long, vertical drop-off shelf that extends out into the middle of the river and is one of the most popular runs for wade fishing on the river.

From Three Mile Access, anglers predominantly wade fish upriver via the 1.3-mile trail maintained by the National Park Service. The Three Mile Islands, located on this trail just up from the boat ramp, mark the water most fished by wade anglers because of the diversity of river features found here. The numerous channels within these islands provide a full day's worth of fishing and trout can frequently be found rising here throughout

Three Mile Access offers wade anglers the most access throughout the river.

the year. These channels are also prime areas for trout to spawn. In the spring and the late fall, please try to avoid walking through and targeting fish on the redds. The land downstream from Three Mile is Crow Tribal land, so stay within the river's high-water mark to avoid trespassing.

While this stretch, by river miles, is only a short 3-mile float, many anglers, especially in the winter and spring, make a full day out of this float, because of the abundance of wade fishing found in these 3 miles. This is also a great float for anglers who only have limited time to fish, often in the early morning or the evening. This section of the river can also be effectively fished in only two to four hours and with the Three Mile ramp only a short row away at any time. Many river users, looking for a full day, choose to put in at the Afterbay and continue on past Three Mile Access all the way down to Bighorn Access, which is 13 miles from Afterbay Access. This longer float is a better option when the river traffic is at its peak.

In the first 3 miles of the river, float anglers will encounter the one significant hazard on the upper river—the Suck Hole. Here an old concrete retaining wall causes a dangerous back eddy. At all costs, do not get sucked into this hazard or get your boat sideways while navigating past this area. Keep your boat straight and stay in the main flow (this may require some forward rowing) to go over a large, smooth mound of water and current, and the current will quickly carry your boat past the concrete wall and the eddy.

Riffles and drop-offs, such as this one around islands, are great places for anglers to find trout. HALE HARRIS

The entire Upper 3 is ideal trout habitat, in which trout thrive on the abundance of food found throughout. Being the closest to the dam, this section of the river is the most stable and goes through the least amount of change from year to year. You can expect to find trout, at one time or another, in every square inch of it.

While not deep, this section of river does offer a fair amount of gradient, which creates riffled runs that give way to several long flats. Each of these runs and flats holds an abundance of trout and is easy for anglers to fish thoroughly. These riffled runs are accentuated by numerous drop-offs, shelves, and inside bends that all hold fish.

Some of the best riffle water is found around several distinct islands throughout this short stretch. Fish routinely feed in the flats above these islands, in the seams at the bottom end, and in the back channels. Anglers should not overlook the flats, located in between these riffles, either. These are areas where trout can feed efficiently. High quantities of food are available in these slow-water areas, and trout also freely rise in many of these flats.

Because of the trout's propensity to sit in the shallows between Afterbay and Three Mile, there is excellent opportunity for anglers to sight-nymph to large trout. Watching the white of a large trout's mouth appear as it takes your fly is one of the most rewarding experiences the Bighorn offers. I always tell my clients to first present their fly along the edges of riffle or other river feature, without ever taking a step into the river, if

Don't overlook any water in this stretch of river—it all holds fish. Here an angler prepares to fish an inside riffle bend. Sow bugs are of the utmost importance when nymphing the Upper 3, shortly followed in importance by midge pupae and *Baetis* nymphs. Each of these food groups takes fish nearly every day of the year when nymph fishing from Afterbay to Three Mile. HALE HARRIS

The Upper 3 sees the most angling pressure on the river for good reason; it holds the most trout per mile and access is abundant. Double hook-ups are common. I often refer to these fish as being on "crack." They simply cannot resist the constant conveyer belt of food coming through their feeding lie. These trout gorge themselves day in and day out, on subsurface food sources especially. PAUL RUHTER

possible. This is a great time to incorporate the use of a shallow water or spring creek nymph rig. When fishing the Upper 3, approach each run with caution and work the water thoroughly. All of the main runs hold large quantities of trout that feed actively.

Catch rates on the Upper 3 with nymphs are often good, regardless of angling pressure. In general, the only times I find the fish go off the bite on the Upper 3 is when they have gorged themselves to a point of extreme satiation, which does happen at times, during heavy emergences of aquatic insects. The other time trout here can go off the bite is when a cold front quickly moves into the area and the barometer is on the drop. However, once these cold fronts stabilize, even if air temperatures have become much colder, the fish seem to go back on the bite rather quickly.

While the above may be true when fishing subsurface imitations, dry-fly anglers will not find the same ease of approach when fishing on the surface in this section of river. This is one of the many fascinating features of the Bighorn: while nymphing can provide some of the easiest fly fishing, fishing drys on the same stretch of water can be some of the most challenging fly fishing found anywhere. Though not always difficult, the Bighorn's trout can be incredibly wary and cautious when feeding on emergers in the surface film or on adults off the surface. A stealthy approach and exacting presentation are the keys to success here.

Fishing with Crowds

Great fishing often attracts a crowd, and for good reason. During peak times of the year, often when insect hatches are at their height, the Bighorn River sees a significant increase in anglers in search of banner fishing days. Managing the crowds is often about managing your expectations as an angler and practicing proper river etiquette.

Luckily the Bighorn River handles angling pressure better than any river I know. While at the busiest of times you may see numerous other anglers in the same stretch of river, everyone still seems to be catching plenty of fish throughout the day. Because of the incredible number of fish per mile and abundant feeding lies for trout on the Bighorn, there is plenty of room for anglers to spread out and find success, especially if they are able to use numerous fishing techniques. There are a few things you can do to avoid these crowds during peak times.

Fish the shoulder seasons. The Bighorn has one of the longest fishing seasons of any river, and early spring and late fall provide some of the best fishing of the year.

Start early or fish late. The river is often the busiest from mid-morning, after anglers have finished breakfast, until late afternoon, when anglers need to get off for dinner at their respective lodge.

Fish the entire river. The upper river from Afterbay to Three Mile and then Three Mile to Bighorn Access are the two busiest stretches of river each day. Many anglers rarely consider the lower river a viable option. While the number of fish per mile isn't nearly as high as below the dam, you can have a quality fishing experience during most of the year.

Double float. By putting your boat in and taking it out twice, you can often get ahead of other boats in the morning and be well behind other boats when you float the second time, essentially creating your own solitude. Many anglers do this by floating Three Mile to Bighorn Access in the morning, then Afterbay Access to Three Mile Access in the afternoon.

Etiquette

As anglers, we all have a different approach to our time on the water, and take enjoyment from different things. I believe we each have a responsibility as anglers to respect the fishery, its trout, and other anglers. In my opinion, there is no place for confrontation on a trout river—a situation that typically only results from a lack of respect for others or complete ignorance. By following the basic rules of river etiquette, everyone can have a quality experience on the river.

Most incidents that occur on the river can be avoided by respecting another angler's space. There is no excuse for walking into another angler's riffle, floating through someone's drift, or casting into another angler's pod of rising fish. There is an incredible abundance of good spots to fish on the Bighorn and excellent water waits around each bend. As a general rule, it is best to show other anglers the amount of space that you would want tobe given to yourself. Conducting yourself in a way that is detrimental to others for the sake of your own benefit is not the best course of action when sharing a public resource with others.

Other incidents can easily be avoided by quickly launching and retrieving your boat, not cutting in front of another floater, not low-holing a wading angler, and not dropping your anchor in the middle of a busy run. It is always the best practice to pull aside and anchor along the bank to either net a fish or to stop and work an area. All in all, practicing basic common sense and practicing good river etiquette will ensure that everyone has an enjoyable experience fly fishing the Bighorn.

As a general rule, acting in a way that allows you to enjoy your experience on the water without detracting from that of others is an honorable way to conduct yourself when making use of a public space. One of the biggest changes that I have seen is the party atmosphere brought to the river now and again by a select few, often at the expense of most anglers. The major offense comes by way of portable speakers used to blast their favorite music as they make their way down the river. While this may be enjoyable for some, not everyone wants to be subjected to music while engaged in the outdoors. The other issue is the need to showboat and let every other angler on the river know that they caught a trout. Enjoying the river experience with others and building a sense of camaraderie is one thing, but shouting and hooting and hollering so every other angler hears you is another. ■

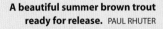

A beautiful summer brown trout ready for release. PAUL RHUTER

Some of the best dry-fly water on the Upper 3 is found on the glassy flats where insects collect and trout can efficiently feed. Here an angler's prey can easily detect an angler's poor presentation or clumsy movements. When fishing slowly moving and flat water areas, such as the Red Cliffs and the lower end of the Landing Strip, trout have the opportunity to use the utmost discretion when deciding whether to select your fly. Light tippets down to 6X, long leaders from 10 to 14 feet, sparsely dressed flies, and a drag-free presentation should always be used for the most success when fishing these flats.

During periods of emergence, fish will move into the riffles and feed more freely, making the angler's opportunities much better. The Landing Strip is a prime example of where you can find fish feeding on the edge of a riffle, as well as both sides of Hot Dog Hole and the inside corner of Dag's Run. The easiest dry-fly fishing occurs during the midst of an emergence when trout pod up to feed on the recently hatched insects and your presentation doesn't have to be as exact.

With consistent flows and stable water temperatures, which come out of the dam in the 40s and low 50s most of the year, hatches of midges and BWOs are the most consistent producers of rising trout in this section of the river. Prolific hatches of these insects come off routinely in this section of river each winter and spring. For this reason, the Bighorn River is one of the most reliable winter and spring fisheries in all of Montana. The Bighorn has a diehard following of winter and spring anglers who fish the Afterbay to Three Mile stretch from February through May.

Flats are an ideal place to find fish feeding on the surface. Patience and a good presentation will usually result in a hookup. HALE HARRIS

The most consistent hatch throughout the summer on the Upper 3 is the Black Caddis hatch. Throughout the day, and especially in the evening, this dark-bodied caddis clouds the air and puts trout in a feeding frenzy. Floating this short stretch of river on a warm summer evening is a great way to avoid the crowds and experience some of the best dry-fly fishing the Bighorn offers.

Summer hatches of Pale Morning Duns, Tan Caddis, and Tricos are also prominent in this section of river, but not reliable every year. Their appearance depends on water temperatures in this stretch closest to the dam. On some years, because of the cold nature of this section of the river, these hatches will come off four to six weeks later than "normal." I have seen Pale Morning Duns in September, Tan Caddis in October, and Tricos into November in this section.

These hatches come off well in the riffles and the trout respond well to them. Even during the most prolific emergences, trout in this section can demand your best presentation. The wariest of trout need to be fooled with your first cast. In many cases you won't get a second or third chance. The nymphal forms of each of these hatches are also just as important as the adult stage in this section of river. Trout will gorge on the nymphs of insects, such as PMDs, Tan Caddis, and Tricos, along the bottom of the river.

While this section of the river is the most pressured water on the Bighorn, the unparalleled number of fish per mile, an aquatic biomass that makes fish grow at alarming rates, and endless river features lead to excellent catch rates almost every day of the year.

THREE MILE TO BIGHORN

The water from Three Mile to Bighorn features many of the same characteristics that make Afterbay to Three Mile so good. This stretch, also known as Three to Thirteen because of the relation of the put-in and take-out to Afterbay Dam in river miles, offers anglers excellent trout habitat and the greatest diversity of fishing opportunity found on the Bighorn.

Walk-in access on this stretch of the river is limited. Walking down from Three Mile is difficult because it is tribal land. Anglers looking to wade fish have to stay within the high-water mark. Bighorn Access provides a good amount of walk-in access upstream of the boat ramps. However, this isn't the best water to be fishing by foot. The advantage that walk-in fishermen have upstream of Bighorn Access is that they don't have to contend with any boat traffic until later in the afternoon, making this a great place to fish in the morning. Anglers wading downstream from the boat ramps should note that the land quickly becomes private.

Anglers putting in at Three Mile will be floating 10 miles downstream to Bighorn Access. Three Mile can be busy in the morning with anglers launching boats, but it is typically not nearly as busy as Afterbay. Anglers

While Three Mile Access (shown here) is a busy place in the morning, anglers quickly spread out as they move downriver due to the abundant variety of water throughout this stretch of the river.

putting in their boats at Three Mile will find that traffic dissipates more quickly as floaters have more room to spread out in this longer stretch of river. Many anglers and guides won't start fishing from the boat right away, but instead will push down to one of the most promising runs in this stretch.

While traffic dissipates quickly in the morning in this section of river, it can also become busy in the afternoon, as floaters from the Upper 3 make their way down to Bighorn Access. Floaters putting in at Three Mile can either stay ahead of this "flotilla" or choose to wade and fish a run and wait for the congestion to move down ahead of them throughout the later part of the day.

Populations of brown and rainbow trout are relatively the same for the first few miles of this float, as up above on the upper 3 miles of river. After the first three or four miles of this stretch, trout populations, while still high and healthy, begin to diminish slightly.

The wider nature of the river in this stretch, along with the lack of access by foot, allows anglers to spread out. This section of the river begins to show more character as it twists and turns through a continually changing landscape. Here you will find a greater diversity of trout holding water than on the upper 3 miles. While I enjoy fishing this stretch from the boat, it is experienced at its best when anglers stop and concentrate their time fishing likely looking water.

In addition to the similar river features found on the Upper 3, such as riffled runs, drop-off shelves, inside bends, and flats, this section offers several large islands, cliffs, a few rapids, and floatable channels that hold excellent populations of trout. Many of these channels are floatable at most water levels throughout the year.

If you are interested in floating these channels, make sure that it is feasible before you do so. It is always best to park at the top and wade fish your way down through it if you are unsure. Take appropriate caution floating a channel at flows under 2,500 cfs. At high water all of these channels become floatable and offer great fishing from a boat. Another thing to keep in mind is that at times a channel may be floatable, but anglers could already be in its prime runs and floating through could ruin their fishing

Quickly after launching, anglers typically find their way into one of the most popular channels on the river, the Snag Channel, on river left, just below the first flat after Three Mile Access. Many times anglers will push down from Three Mile to get into the most popular channels on this stretch of river, such as Snag, Duck Blind, Corral, and Schneider's Channels. These channels are smaller than the main channel, have concentrated populations of trout, and are much more manageable to fish.

The first half of this float offers exceptional features and is often the focus of most anglers' attentions. Popular areas of this stretch that offer an abundance of wade fishing opportunity include Snag Channel, Duck Blind Channel, S. B. A, Crow Beach, Corral, and both sides of the river in front of the Bighorn Club, each offering excellent fishing each day. It is also beneficial to fish while floating between these key areas.

Side channels such as this one offer anglers solitude and great fishing in more intimate surroundings. Don't overlook side channels and sloughs of any size—they all hold fish.
JAY NICHOLS

Many anglers only focus on the most obvious water in this stretch, yet nice fish such as the one pictured are found in water often overlooked by most anglers. The scud produces in just about every water type found on the Bighorn. PAT DORSEY

The Three Mile to Bighorn Access section (3 to B) is a transition zone between the upper and lower river. The further you move down in this stretch the more the river changes. The river begins to show characteristics of both the upper and lower river in the second half of this float. While not as straightforward as the first half of the float, anglers that know how to read water will have excellent fishing all the way down to Bighorn Access.

The only limitation anglers find when fishing the second half of this stretch is floating grass, which becomes an issue when change in the daily flow dislodges grass from the river edges and carries it into the main flow. The accumulation of floating grass seems to compound in the lower half of the 3 to B stretch and can make fishing more challenging when anglers are forced to routinely clean moss from their flies. Unfortunately, it's not possible to predict when this will occur.

With a lack of development on this stretch of the river, two main houses provide good reference points when floating this stretch. The Bighorn Club, a large time-share fishing club on river right, is a good halfway point when floating the upper 13 river miles from Afterbay to Bighorn Access. The next is Mike Craig's house, on river right, just below the Three Rivers area. This house is a good marker that you are two-thirds of the way to the take-out. Many people find themselves rowing to the boat ramp in the dark from here when evening hatches have caused them to lose track of time.

Throughout the summer, water temperatures from Three Mile to Bighorn Access typically fall perfectly in the 55- to 65-degree temperature range, which are highly conducive to prolific insect emergences and promote a high rate of metabolism in the trout, keeping them active and receptive to flies.

While the biomass may not be as dense as it is on the upper 3 miles, the diversity of aquatic insects that contribute to an angler's success may be greater. In addition to a large population of crustaceans, aquatic worms, and midges, slightly warmer water temperatures in this section also produce consistent mayfly, caddis, and stonefly hatches that provide excellent match-the-hatch dry-fly fishing.

In addition to a great Black Caddis hatch, similar in timing and intensity to that found on the Upper 3, this section offers the best Tan Caddis hatch on the river. These large *Hydropsyche* caddis allow the trout to feed throughout the day on the larva, pupa, adult, and egg-laying stages of this hatch. When conditions are right, the Tan Caddis hatch can last for several months, well into September and, sometimes, even into October.

Because of the distance between access points, many anglers choose to float fish this section of the river in between wade spots. Fishing from your boat, between wade fishing the best spots, is a highly efficient way of approaching the water down to the Thirteen Mile (Bighorn) Access. JAY NICHOLS

The well-oxygenated runs found here also produce excellent hatches of the only stonefly species found on the Bighorn, the Little Yellow Sally. Occurring from the end of June through July and emerging in the mid-morning to afternoon, this size 12 to 14 stonefly gets the trout's attention below and on the surface. This is the one hatch where we often deviate from the norm and fish flashy beadhead nymph patterns with great success. I often fish a Yellow Sally nymph as a point fly, with a caddis pupa or mayfly nymph as a trailing fly, during the length of this hatch, especially in fast water runs.

Terrestrials also work well in this stretch throughout the summer. With less angling pressure and more water to fish, in comparison with the Upper 3, there is more undisturbed water in which fish will eat ants, beetles, and grasshoppers opportunistically. I routinely fish this stretch with a dry-dropper rig from the boat, in between wade spots, with great success.

Because of the length of this stretch, this is also a great float for fishing streamers. While predominantly used in the fall, streamers can work well in this stretch year-round. The fish in the lower end of this stretch of water seem to be especially susceptible to a well-presented streamer. Intermediate sinking lines are ideal for fishing streamers in this stretch of water.

During high-water and runoff conditions, Mountain Pocket Creek, located below the Bighorn Club, and Soap Creek can bring in significant amounts of dirty water to this stretch of the river. Both of these creeks come in from river right and rarely muddy the whole river. The left half of the river typically remains fishable down to Bighorn Access. Mountain

Streamers work well on this stretch of river throughout the year for trout of all sizes. Don't overlook streamer fishing during the spring and summer, especially in this stretch.
JAY NICHOLS

The Drive-in or car bodies is a famous landmark within this stretch of the river made famous by the Simms Fishing Products ad from the late 90s. While out of the ordinary, the cars provided an effective form of bank stabilization. DAVID PALMER

Pocket clears quickly, while during the worst years Soap Creek can run muddy for several weeks.

Anglers floating this stretch will take out at Bighorn Access. Throughout this 10-mile float, there is only one area of concern to novice oarsmen. The Bighorn Rapids are down the left channel after the long run and flat along the Grey Cliffs. This rapid, while turbid for the Bighorn, should not be of worry for experienced oarsmen. Novice oarsmen need to keep their boat straight and slightly to the right of the main waves during this short section of wave trains.

This 10-mile stretch of water, from Three Mile Access to Bighorn Access, is a favorite of veteran Bighorn River anglers and guides because of the diversity it offers. An angler can often find totally different fishing situations in the same day throughout this long stretch of water. While many anglers only key in on the most obvious runs in the section, there are numerous secondary "B" and "C" spots in this section that fish well. Fish thoroughly and don't overlook any of the water; some of the best water here is the least obvious. With the greater diversity of water, there are far more micro spots, or secondary holding water, in addition to prime runs in this stretch of water to find rising trout. Observant anglers, who read the water the best, are often rewarded with the best dry-fly fishing and sight-nymphing opportunities throughout this stretch.

The Lower River

The river from Bighorn Access to Two Leggins is often referred to as the lower river and receives only a fraction of the angling pressure the upper river does. This is mostly due to the lower population of fish per mile (1,500 to 2,500, with numbers decreasing as you travel downriver), fewer aquatic insect hatches, and distance from Fort Smith. The river here also has more varied river conditions that are harder for some to read and less reliable insect hatches; with that said, it still offers first-class fishing throughout the year and has more trout per mile than many of the other great trout rivers in Montana.

Visiting anglers looking to fish a diversity of water will appreciate this lower stretch of river. This section offers a greater chance of solitude and the ability to use different tactics, in contrast to the upper river. Anglers visiting the Bighorn should look at it as getting two rivers for the price of one. Hiring a guide who specializes in the lower river is a great way to learn the nuances of the lower river and add diversity to your fishing trip.

The lower river pictured here at Mallard's Landing Access is wider and flatter than the upper river and receives far less angling pressure. DAVID PALMER

Anglers fish the lower river to find solitude. The river features here are less obvious. Anglers should use the boat to cover water until they come upon a good spot to wade fish to a rising trout. These opportunities are usually found in side channels or around islands in this stretch. JAY NICHOLS

There are two distinct lower river floats: Bighorn Access to Mallard's Landing is 9 river miles, and Mallard's Landing to Two Leggins is 10.7 miles. Camping is permitted at all three of these fishing access sites, and a two-day float with overnight camping at Mallard's Landing is a great way to experience the lower river. Motorized watercraft are allowed below Bighorn Access and, at times, can be a nuisance to anglers, most noticeably while dry-fly fishing the main channel. Fishing with live bait is also permitted from Bighorn Access to its confluence with the Yellowstone.

The main river, below Bighorn Access, begins to flatten out as the river valley widens. Here the main river is wider and deep runs give way to long flats. Heavily braided sections that feature numerous side channels break up these long runs, some of which are floatable and some not. Every bank and feature throughout this stretch doesn't necessarily fish well, like on the upper river. It takes time to figure out the nuances of the lower river and to learn which runs hold the most fish. Taking the time to fish it thoroughly and focusing on the riffled runs are good places to start.

Most of the best water on the lower river is found in the numerous side channels and extensive river braids. Not every channel is created equal and time spent out of the boat, exploring the finest looking water, is the best way to find a few of the large trout that call these channels home. Most of these side channels are floatable and can be fished effectively from the boat. The lower river in general, because of its size, fishes well from a boat, as you can cover as much water as possible.

The lower river doesn't fish consistently year-round like the upper river does, mostly due to variable water conditions. Water temperatures on the lower river can be, on average, anywhere from six to ten degrees warmer than when it comes over Afterbay Dam. Consequently, insect hatches start about two weeks ahead of the upper river.

Conversely, during the dog days of summer, water temperatures can become stressful for trout. This is not always the case, but does happen during warmer than average summers. Once the water approaches 70 degrees, it is wise to fish elsewhere. There is no need for anglers to add stress to the fish by making them fight for their lives. As summer wanes, fall water temperatures will come down to more suitable temperatures.

Unlike the upper river, which is protected by the dam, the lower river can be negatively impacted by spring runoff and irrigation returns that can turn it off-color. Soap Creek and Rotten Grass Creek are the main contributors of muddy spring runoff on the Lower Bighorn. Rotten Grass Creek, especially, can stay off-color for extended periods of time. Irrigation return water from when farmers flood their agricultural land adjacent to the river can muddy the river at times also. The lower river can become unfishable for extended periods of time, especially during spring runoff. Early spring, right up until runoff, and early summer, after runoff, are great times to fish this lower river. Consult with one of the fly shops for current conditions or check the water clarity by driving over the St. Xavier or Two Leggins bridges.

Regardless of the time of year I am fishing on the lower river, I am typically not focused on the number of fish I catch, but the size of the fish I catch. Longtime Bighorn outfitters, such as Joe Caton and Dave Schouff,

have made their living on the lower river for more than twenty-five years. They consistently catch trout over 24 inches out of this stretch of river each year.

Because of the more silted river bottom, scuds and sow bugs are not as dense as they are farther upstream. Trout still feed on them routinely, but at times they are not as important a food as aquatic worms, which trout feed on in this stretch throughout

An angler casts to rising fish in a lower river side channel. This section of the river is easily wet waded throughout the summer. Here anglers can break the river down into a small-stream atmosphere.

This hefty rainbow was caught on a San Juan Worm fished through a riffle. Many of the largest rainbows down there are taken on worm imitations throughout the seasons. While nymph fishing the lower river, I often set up my standard nymph rig with a worm imitation on top and a sow bug or generic mayfly nymph below. ERIC WILCOX

the year. Mayfly, caddis, and stonefly hatches occur in this stretch, just not with the same density or diversity as found above, and they generally have a shorter period of seasonal emergence.

In general, because of a lower abundance of food and overall less angling pressure, trout in the lower river can be less selective and feed more opportunistically. Nymph fishing is always good throughout this stretch. Anglers should focus on inside bends, riffles, and drop-offs when fishing from the boat. Wading the side channels and nymph fishing throughout this stretch is also a good tactic. The standard Bighorn River indicator nymph rig is the best setup for this water. Changing your weight and the depth of your strike indicator will get you the best results, since there is a wide array of river features throughout this stretch. In general I tend to fish my nymph rigs a foot or two shorter down here than the upper river, mostly to get my flies down more quickly over the abundant drop-offs.

The lower river features the kind of water that keeps streamer fishermen intrigued continually, because the water looks as if it could hold a true trophy throughout its length. Seven- and eight-weight rods, with full sinking lines, allow me to work the deep drop-offs, fast-water banks, and the middle of the river equally well. You won't always move a giant, but dedicated streamer fishermen can routinely catch nice trout. Streamers allow you to cover a lot of water, which seems to help in this stretch where I feel that trout are more likely to forage on larger food, such as other fish, large terrestrials, aquatic worms, leeches, and hellgrammites.

When fishing the lower river on the surface, I often find the best success comes from prospecting with dry-fly attractors and terrestrial imitations that are suggestive of a wide variety of insects. Trout in the lower river generally feed opportunistically, but in the spring and fall, Blue-Winged Olives bring nice-sized pods of trout to the surface, though the hatch is not nearly as consistent or as long in duration as the emergence on the upper river. Also, these hatches are not as widespread throughout the lower river either. You may see a pod of fish in one area and not see rising fish for another few miles. During the spring and fall, I enjoy fishing streamers from the boat until finding rising trout on the surface. Once I locate fish feeding on BWOs, I will set up on the fish, either by anchoring the boat mid-river or by wading. In the late spring, anglers on the lower river can also happen upon a hatch of Mother's Day Caddis. This large (#14-16) caddis can create excellent surface activity. It is not dependable each year, but something for anglers to be aware of.

Throughout the summer, hatches of Pale Morning Duns, Yellow Sallies, and Tricos bring trout to the surface. The best summer dry-fly fishing can be had from when runoff subsides to when water temperatures reach the 70-degree mark. The Pale Morning Dun and Yellow Sally hatches will bring trout to the surface in pods, but blind-fishing patterns imitating these naturals is highly effective. Tricos provide the best match-the-hatch dry-fly

This brown trout measuring nearly 24 inches and caught by Charlie Mcloughlin was taken on a Tan Caddis dry fly in the Mallard's to Two Leggins stretch. PETE SHANAFELT

fishing in the summer from Bighorn Access to Two Leggins, with heavy emergences occurring each year. We have anglers coming into the fly shop routinely throughout the summer complaining about the lack of Tricos on the upper river. The truth is they are typically emerging prolifically on the lower river.

Dry-fly fishing comes to life on the lower river when trout aggressively look for big meals on top, such as grasshoppers, crickets, ants, and beetles throughout the summer. With the lack of aquatic insect density that is found in the upper river, trout in the lower river will readily feed on the surface. A terrestrial fished as the dry fly in a dry-dropper rig or as a point fly in a two-dry-fly rig is often my most used tactic in this stretch of river. A hopper with an ant, or ant with a Yellow Sally dry, or a hopper with a Tungsten Split Case PMD are all effective examples of dry-fly setups. Incorporating a twitching motion to your terrestrial imitation adds a life-like element to your imitation and often elicits aggressive strikes on the lower river.

As you near the end of this stretch of river you will come across the Two Leggins diversion dam. The dam will be right after an old abandoned bridge, located at the end of a long flat. You will have plenty of time to set up for navigating this obstacle. Right after the diversion dam the river splits into two channels. Enter the left channel, center yourself in the channel, and keep your boat straight. You will ride easily over the diversion dam. After floating over the diversion dam, the boat ramp is on river left on the upstream side of the Highway 313 Bridge.

CHAPTER 5

Fish Food and Fly Patterns

The Bighorn River is home to a large and diverse biomass consisting of insects and aquatic organisms that thrive in its nutrient-rich waters and terrestrials that flourish on the land bordering the river. This diversity and abundance of food available to the trout are what make the Bighorn River the spectacular trout fishery that it is. The hatches produced by the stable tailwater flows not only sustain the healthy populations of trout but also provide tremendous angling opportunity.

This plentiful supply of food consists of crustaceans, annelids (worms), and smaller fish as well as numerous aquatic and terrestrial insects. These all take a varying prominence in the trout diet, depending on the time of year and river conditions. To pick the right fly that will represent what the trout are eating with the most enthusiasm, it is important to understand the key characteristics of each of these food sources.

While casting to trout feeding on an emerging insect is arguably the height of our sport, on the Bighorn it is the crustaceans such as aquatic sow bugs and scud (freshwater shrimp) and worms that supply a steady amount of food to feeding trout and yield dynamic year-round nymph fishing. Crustaceans and worms thrive in the alkaline water with high mineral content and plentiful plant life.

For larger, predator trout, smaller fish will also supply a part—or sometimes all—of their diet. With the high recruitment of juvenile fish from year to year on the Bighorn, brown and rainbow trout, along with juvenile whitefish, are a major source of nourishment on the Bighorn.

The Bighorn offers a tremendous diversity and abundance of aquatic insects such as caddis, mayflies, midges, and stoneflies as well as terrestrials. These "hatches" are what draw dry-fly anglers to this river, which has one of the longest dry-fly seasons in Montana. The Bighorn, like other tailwater rivers and spring creeks, produces insect hatches that offer relatively less diversity of available insects, yet the insects present emerge in far greater abundance and for longer periods of time.

Trout feed on non-hatches such as sow bugs, scuds, and annelids year-round. These food sources account for the trout's tremendous growth rates. PAT DORSEY

Most aquatic insect hatches that occur on the Bighorn are represented with fly imitations that range in size from 16 to 20. When imitating these small hatches on the Bighorn, with nymphs or dry flies, matching the size of the natural is crucial. While small in size, these insects hatch in such large quantities, at times, that trout will feed ferociously on them. Anglers shouldn't be intimidated by fishing small flies to imitate these insects. While a certain level of casting proficiency is necessary, persistence and patience are the most important aspects.

Many of these hatches can overlap and any number of them could be present at any period of time. We often see this in the spring with midges and Blue-Winged Olives, in the summer with PMDs, Sallies, and Black Caddis, and again in the fall with Tricos and Pseudos. These scenarios present their own sets of challenges, and understanding these emergences will better help you prepare for your time on the water.

While these ideal conditions exist, certain variables affect the density and availability of insects and other aquatic organisms from one year to

Tricos are representative of insects found on the Bighorn and other tailwater fisheries. While small in size, most of their emergences are prolific and seasonal hatch periods are longer in duration. JAY NICHOLS

Because of the sheer abundance and diversity of food in the Bighorn, anglers can usually find actively feeding fish along the bottom or on the surface.
HALE HARRIS

the next. Water releases (determined by reservoir levels), sediment load, and, especially, water temperature all have significant impacts on the timing and availability of hatches from year to year. During the severe drought years of the late 1990s and early 2000s, many of the key mayfly, caddis, and stonefly hatches in the upper river nearly ceased to exist due to consecutive years of below average flows. These low flows caused a thick bed of sediment to blanket the bottom of the river and choke out the abundant populations of aquatic insects. After the recent three consecutive years of high water—from 2009 through 2011—the river was cleansed of the sediment that had blanketed the river bottom. As a result, aquatic insect diversity and population once again thrived. Furthermore, the amounts of aquatic vegetation and sediment found in the river seem to be two of the most evident variables that dictate the abundance of crustaceans within the river ecosystem.

Yearly fluctuations in water temperature can drastically affect the timing of insect hatches. Because of the bottom-release dam system, which has the outlet from a reservoir that exceeds 300 feet in depth, we are more likely to encounter colder than normal temperatures when flows are normal or low. Conversely, water temperatures do not usually rise quickly, so insects do not typically emerge prematurely. I have seen Blue-Winged Olives hatch from March straight through until August, Tricos hatch well into November, Sallies hatch in high-water years in June and, in low, cold-water years, not until September, and Tan Caddis that don't show up on the upper river until the end of October.

On the Bighorn, there is rarely a down time in the feeding rhythms of the trout, unlike what is often found on freestone rivers. Having also guided on many freestone rivers, I have often found a "window" each day when the fishing is especially good, depending on the insect emergence or food available to them. On these freestone rivers, there may be three to four hours during the course of the day when an abundance of food is available. During the other twenty hours of the day, there is much less food readily available. The trout become conditioned to this rhythm, adapt their feeding cycles to it, and typically offer good angling opportunity only during this window.

I find that because of the large abundance of food and the diversity of organisms found throughout the Bighorn, we don't get these drastic changes in feeding behavior as frequently. There are most certainly exceptions to this rule. During the most intense period of the daily emergences, you will definitely see an increase in feeding activity, but in general, we typically only encounter a few periods of "slow" fishing on the Bighorn—slow being a relative term when talking about this river. This sometimes happens when a hatch cycle is tailing off or has just ended, or before or after an intense emergence.

Building a Bighorn Fly Box

Bighorn trout are often exposed to a near constant drift of food throughout the water column, and often respond to any item that looks and acts like food. To take advantage of this, I carry a wide array of impressionistic fly patterns such as Pheasant Tail Nymphs and Parachute Adams that are vague representations of an insect, or patterns that represent characteristics of more than one insect and give the impression of life to the fish.

On the flip side, when trout in the Bighorn are selectively feeding, they key into a specific attribute of an insect or organism when an abundance and diversity of food are available. This selective feeding is evident during

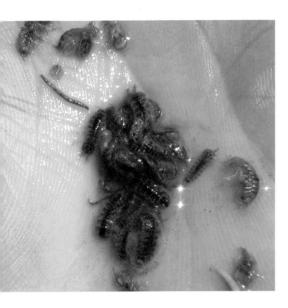

A stomach pump can show you what the trout are feeding on. In this case trout were feeding selectively on sow bugs. This trout also opportunistically fed on a few red midge larvae and a scud.

the PMD emergence, when trout are keying in on the split back stage of the hatch. At this time, dark-bodied PMD nymphs are ascending to the surface with their wing case split, displaying a bright yellow spot in their thorax. The Split Case PMD nymph is a perfect example of an imitative fly pattern that was created to imitate this specific stage. During times when fish are feeding selectively like this and you choose the right imitative pattern, you will often rack up large catch rates of trout on the Bighorn.

Fishing on the Bighorn can become technical also, especially when trout become conditioned to how a natural should act and look. At this time, pattern selection becomes that much more important. Bighorn fish may see the same insect hatch day in and day out for weeks or months at a time. The Black Caddis hatch is a prime example of this. By the end of this hatch, I may be using different dry-fly patterns and sizes from when the hatch started.

With that said, you could have success with an assortment of flies only consisting of a dozen generic nymphs. However, with all the food available to the trout at any given time on the Bighorn, the fish can become selective to a particular pattern. Having a wide variety of patterns that are both imitative and generic is highly recommended. Selecting the right fly pattern can mean the difference between having a mediocre day or a banner day. With the sometimes-close nature of the fishing between anglers on the Bighorn, it is often evident who has figured out the day's "hot fly."

Understanding which food sources are available to the trout and understanding the life cycle of an insect are the most important aspects of building an effective Bighorn River fly box. Walking into a fly shop and asking, "What's working?" will only take you so far. The more you know

Guide Seth Byler chooses a fly from one of his nymph boxes that includes scuds and sow bugs. DAVID PALMER

about the characteristics of an insect emergence, the more success you will have as an angler. There is a certain art to building a fly box. Being organized on the river and having a fly assortment that allows you to make an accurate fly pattern selection for any situation you may encounter are crucial to your success.

The number of fly boxes that an angler carries will always vary from one angler to the next, but I would rather be overprepared than not have the right fly. For me, I organize my flies specifically by each hatch or organism that I encounter on the Bighorn. Some of these, depending on the importance of the hatch, receive multiple boxes. The number of patterns I carry within those boxes depends on the intensity and duration of the hatch or how long the organism is available to the trout. I will go into greater detail about this when I break down each food source and the patterns that represent each one successfully.

In my system, PMDs, Sallies, Tricos, Black Caddis, and Tan Caddis all receive their own box, containing flies that cover each stage of the insect's emergence. I have two boxes for the Blue-Winged Olive and midge emergences, one with surface patterns and the other with subsurface patterns. To round out my dry-fly patterns, I also carry two terrestrial boxes: one for ants and beetles and another for hoppers. I then carry a box for worms, a box for generic nymphs, a box for sow bugs, and a box for scuds. To round out my subsurface collection, I carry two large streamer boxes: one for generic streamers such as Woolly Buggers and Zonkers and another for specialty streamers. What I carry is certainly on the extreme end of what anyone needs to carry but, if kept organized, it is an easy arrangement to navigate.

I recommend carrying a few good patterns to mimic each stage of a hatch and finding a fly pattern style that you have had success with and carrying those to imitate every insect species you will encounter. For example, a CDC Sparkle Dun is my most effective mayfly imitation I carry on the Bighorn. Because of this, I adjust the size and color of this pattern for each mayfly hatch—BWOs, Pseudos, Tricos, and PMDs.

Once you have put together a core selection of flies for each food group, use this as a foundation. From there you can begin to experiment with more highly specialized, niche-specific fly patterns. If you are new to fly fishing, or to a particular hatch, ask an expert in a fly shop to create an assortment for you of their favorite flies for mimicking each stage of the hatch. You will be able to build on your base of flies each time you visit the river, depending on the specific needs of the time of year.

Small mayfly nymphs such as Pheasant Tails and Quill Nymphs are staples on the Bighorn River throughout the year. Anglers should also be prepared to fish midges year-round. Carry Zebra Midges in a variety of colors such as black, brown, cream, and red to imitate the larvae present when you are fishing. ASHLEY GARRISON

Below is a compilation of my most successful patterns that have become staples over the years and are found in large quantities in my fly boxes. A few of these patterns are specialized and imitate a specific fishing situation throughout the course of the year, but most of these patterns can be used routinely for each hatch.

CRUSTACEANS: SCUDS AND SOW BUGS

Your crustacean box will consist of scuds and sow bugs. You can never have too many sow bug (#14-20) and scud patterns (#12-16) when fishing the Bighorn. Sow bugs are abundant, and fish feed opportunistically on them year-round and can key in on them selectively at any given time. Sow bugs are especially important when other food sources are not as prevalent. The most important variable to account for is color. Popular sow bug and scud colors include gray, tan, orange, and pink.

Scuds

Scuds, or freshwater shrimp, are available to trout year-round and are especially abundant in the spring (also when other food sources are less abundant) and during high-water years, when they are dislodged from aquatic vegetation. Scuds swim on their side and are known as "side-swimmers" because of the curved shape of their body. Orange and pink scud imitations are the most effective colors on the river. Three theories advanced to explain this are that when scuds die they change to an orange color (as can be seen from trout stomach samples), that the females have an orange/pink "hot spot" in the middle of their body when pregnant, and that a scud turns an orange and/or pink color after molting. Whatever the explanation, as an angler, it is important to know that Bighorn trout have a fondness for orange or pink imitations more than any other colors. Another explanation that I have heard during the spring season is that the trout are not taking a scud imitation as a scud at all, but rather as an egg. Scuds can be found in the Bighorn as large as size 10 and as small as size 18. Most of your patterns for this crustacean should be size 14 to 16.

At times orange scud patterns are irresistible to Bighorn trout. This color change is believed to occur when scuds die or shed their exoskeleton.
JIM SCHOLLMEYER

Bighorn Scud

Hook:	#10-18 Dai-Riki 135
Thread:	Red 6/0 Uni
Rib:	Gold UTC Wire (Brassie)
Back:	Mylar tinsel
Body:	Bighorn orange (shown) or Bighorn pink Wapsi Sow Scud dubbing

Note: Originally designed by Quill Gordon Fly Shop owner Gordon Rose, the Bighorn Scud has been a staple since the 80s. Fish it as a top fly with a midge or Blue-Winged Olive nymph below it. Fish often take this fly as an egg in the spring when rainbow trout are spawning. I like to fish this in larger sizes 10 and 12 during higher water and tied a little thicker in the body. I use size 14 and 16 during low or normal water conditions tied sparse. It works well in both pink and orange.

Berg's Bighorn Scud

Hook:	#14-18 Daiichi 1120
Thread:	Fire orange 6/0 Uni
Body:	Fl. orange, amber, coral (20%/50%/30%) Hareline Dubbin
Overbody:	Mylar tinsel
Rib:	Gold UTC Wire

Note: Tied by Bighorn guide Adam Berg, the key to this bug is the slenderness of the body, its dubbing blend, and just the right amount of flash. This is a favorite winter and spring pattern for many guides. The best colors are orange and pink (substitute the fluorescent orange dubbing for fluorescent pink in the above recipe).

Soft-Hackle Ray Charles

Hook:	#14-20 Dai-Riki 075
Thread:	Fire orange 8/0 Uni
Hackle:	Dun hen
Body:	Gray ostrich herl
Back:	Mylar tinsel
Rib:	Silver wire

Note: The Soft-Hackle Ray Charles works well at imitating both sow bugs and scuds. The soft-hackle on the front gives the fly more motion in the water and the presence of movement, similar to the legs on the naturals. The ostrich herl has a lifelike impression in the water as well. Carry these in gray, pink, and tan. Use the same recipe as above—just change the color of the ostrich herl.

Firebead Soft-Hackle Ray Charles

Hook:	#14-18 Dai-Riki 075
Bead:	Orange Spirit River brass hot bead
Thread:	Fire orange 8/0 Uni
Hackle:	Dun hen neck
Body:	Ostrich herl
Back:	Mylar tinsel
Rib:	Silver wire

Note: The addition of the bright orange Spirit River hot bead to the Soft-Hackle Ray Charles has been incredibly effective over the past few years. It seems to work especially well in the spring and during high water. The beads are also available in tungsten from Spirit River and will help get your flies down even faster. The trout are often responding to the bead as an egg during the spring when the rainbow eggs can be found drifting in the water column. This pattern is becoming increasingly popular throughout the year on the Bighorn.

Sow Bugs

The aquatic sow bug has seven pairs of legs and lives on the river bottom, feeding on aquatic vegetation. These crustaceans are—year in and year out—the most important source of food for Bighorn trout. Many of the guides on the Bighorn always fish a sow bug imitation as their top fly, and the river's most popular pattern, the Ray Charles, still catches trout every day of the year. Sow bugs are particularly important when there is a lack of other food available to the trout. This is especially true in early spring and again in June, which is typically a transition period between the spring and summer insect emergences.

While every sow bug that I have ever collected from my stomach pump or seine is gray with a dark stripe down its back, trout readily take pink, tan, and gray imitations. The one thing that I do often notice is that, from time to time, the tone and width of the band changes. Different imitations account for this. The reasoning behind why the trout take one color sow bug imitation over another is beyond my comprehension at this time. I have asked numerous experts and have never received a concrete answer. All I know is that as an angler, you need to carry all of the colors mentioned above and have them in sizes 14 to 20 every day of the year. Pink sow bugs tend to work really well in the peak of summer when bright sun is a constant, and gray seems to work especially well in the spring. There might be something to this but it certainly is not a rule to live by. The color of your imitation that the fish are eating can change from day to day or week to week. Asking someone in one of the local fly shops is a great idea before hitting the water, since they will often know which color has been most effective recently.

Sow bugs are available to Bighorn trout every day of the year, and they are the most important crustacean for fly fishers to imitate. JIM SCHOLLMEYER

Ray Charles

Hook:	#14-20 Dai-Riki 075
Thread:	Fire orange 8/0 Uni
Rib:	Silver UTC (optional)
Body:	Gray ostrich herl
Back:	Mylar tinsel

Note: The Ray Charles is the most widely fished fly on the Bighorn. It is a simple sow bug imitation that catches countless trout every day of the year. It is effective in gray, pink, and tan.

Soft-Hackle Sow Bug

Hook:	#14-20 Dai-Riki 075
Thread:	Fire orange 8/0 Uni
Hackle:	Dun hen neck
Body:	Shrimp pink Wapsi Antron Dubbing

Note: It is believed that the true effectiveness of this pattern comes from the UV quality that the fire orange thread provides, which presumably makes it easier for the trout to see underwater. It is best to take advantage of this quality by sparsely dubbing the body of this pattern, so that when the pattern becomes wet, the thread shows through. It is an effective sow bug imitation in pink and tan year-round, especially during the summer. In addition to the dubbing listed above, the fly can be tied using tan Sow Scud Dubbing and Hendrickson pink Superfine dubbing. It also comes in a firebead version that fishes well in the spring.

Bighorn Killer Bug

Hook:	#14-18 Dai-Riki 075 or Daiichi 1130
Thread:	Fire orange 8/0 Uni
Body:	Oyster Killer Bug Yarn
Tag:	Red UTC Wire (optional)

Note: This modern spinoff of Frank Sawyer's original Killer Bug has become an effective scud and sow bug imitation throughout the year. The key to this pattern is having the right yarn that produces a shaggy, iridescent look in the water. Once wet, the contrasting colors found in the yarn seem to come alive, making the fly look much different wet than when it is dry. The yarn is available for purchase at the Bighorn Angler.

Poxyback Sow Bug

Hook:	#14-18 Dai-Riki 075
Thread:	Gray 8/0 Uni
Dubbing:	Gray Sow Scud
Flash:	Mylar tinsel or black holographic tinsel
Back:	5-minute epoxy

Note: The hard, reflective epoxy coating on the back of this fly, the scraggly dubbing, and the overall flat nature of this fly make it a great sow bug imitation. I find that this pattern works especially well in bright conditions when sunlight is penetrating the water column. It works well in pink, orange, and gray.

AQUATIC WORMS

Worms (annelids) thrive in the bank soil and in the sediment on the Bighorn's river bottom. They will catch fish every day of the year and are especially important in the lower river, where more sediment is found. The lower river has a higher density of annelids and a lower density of aquatic insects compared to the upper river, so trout feast on worms readily down there. Large rainbows in this lower section seem to be particularly susceptible to well-presented worm imitations.

It seems like over the years the sizes of worm imitations have become smaller, and "micro" worms in solid and two-tone colors have become effective. Annelids are found in a wide variety of colors and sizes. One of the main characteristics of annelids is that they have a colored segment in their body. This colored area seems to be a trigger to the trout and is represented in many of the worm patterns you will find. Aquatic worms can be found in a wide array of sizes. Their imitations are represented by sizes ranging from 4 to 16. Effective colors include brown, wine, red, purple, and orange.

I particularly like a micro worm tied with wine chenille and an orange thread underbody, or a two-tone worm with a light brown and dark brown chenille body with an orange segment in the middle. The wire worm is a highly effective worm pattern, especially in high water because of its weight.

I recommend keeping your assortment of worms fairly basic. A few sizes and colors of each worm style will do the job. Worms can yield excellent results any time of the year, but I find them especially effective in the summer and early fall. You should carry chenille worms (aka San Juan Worms) in a few solid colors and a few two-tone variations. The two-tone combination that I like best is red and brown. Have a few wire worms in your box. These are especially effective in high-water years and help get your flies down in faster water.

Bighorn trout key in on aquatic worms when they are available. Seining the river is a great way to become alert to their presence. JIM SCHOLLMEYER

San Juan Worm

Hook: #8-14 Dai-Riki 135
Thread: Red Danville Waxed
           Flymaster Plus
Body: Red Ultra Chenille

Note: This San Juan Worm works everywhere trout swim. While trout readily take solid-colored worms tied in red, wine, purple, orange, and brown, the two-tone variation is tied using two colors of chenille. It is effective at catching trout on the Bighorn throughout the year. I like to use a combination of wine and brown chenille most often when fishing two-tone worms. Other effective two-tone color combinations are light brown and red, orange and brown, and red and brown.

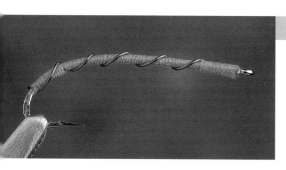

Atomic Worm

Hook: #6-10 Daiichi 1270
Body: Red Glo-Bright Floss #5
Rib: Red UTC Wire (medium)

Note: The unique shape of the Atomic Worm and its large rib make it effective. If you bend the shank of the hook, it gives this worm a more lifelike motion in the water and is believed to account for more hookups.

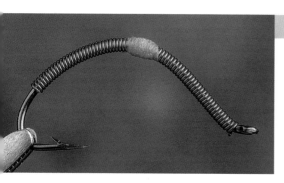

Wire Worm

Hook: #4-8 Mustad 37160
Body: Red 26-gauge craft store
           wire
Thread: Fire orange 3/0 Uni

Note: This worm is tied on an old English bait hook and is highly effective. We tie these using both orange and red wire. Many guides fish this as a top fly because it is heavy and gets down to the bottom quickly. Pinch the barb on this fly to minimize damage to fish. It is especially effective during higher flows.

BAITFISH AND LEECHES

One of the best ways to catch the larger rainbow and brown trout that live in the Bighorn is with a streamer. Streamers are effective year-round, but are most effective in the spring, as the trout's metabolism begins to rise, and again in the fall, when the browns are approaching their spawning season and both breeds are bulking up for winter.

With the large recruitment of yearling fish each year, trout in the Bighorn become accustomed to predation on smaller fish at a young age. Not only do larger fish in the 18- to 24-inch range regularly feast on smaller fish, so do the 14-inch brown trout. Juvenile whitefish, suckers, carp, rainbow trout, brown trout, goldeye, and leeches all provide a forage base for larger trout in the Bighorn.

The Bighorn doesn't have a large population of crayfish like many other tailwaters, but it does contain a large population of leeches. Leech patterns such as the Woolly Bugger, which is as good as any fished slowly on the bottom of the river, can be highly effective. With all the sediment found in the lower river, and slightly warmer water temperatures, leeches thrive. I have been wet wading on the lower river in the summer and found leeches stuck to my feet after getting back in the boat. Some of them are also small enough to be taken as samples in your stomach pump.

Your baitfish or streamer box should consist of single and articulated patterns that represent a variety of pattern silhouettes that each move and act in their own unique way. Examples of these silhouettes include Woolly Buggers, Zonkers, and Clousers. The streamer world is saturated with hundreds of different patterns—there is typically always some hot newcomer to the market that is good to have. The patterns highlighted here are staples that seem to work year in and year out. Once you have a core set of silhouettes, carry each one in a variety of sizes and colors. Size should range from 1/0 to 12 and your colors should include olive, black, olive/black, olive/white, white, and yellow/brown. You should also have a good mix of simple drab patterns and flashy patterns in all of the color combinations mentioned above.

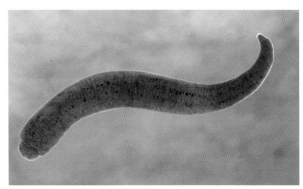

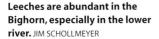

Leeches are abundant in the Bighorn, especially in the lower river. JIM SCHOLLMEYER

Conehead Woolly Bugger

Hook: #2-8 Dai-Riki 710
Thread: Black 6/0 Uni
Cone: Gold 5.5 mm cone
Body: Black peacock Estaz
            #1312 (medium)
Legs: Black/blue flake Crazy
            Legs (optional)
Hackle: Black Woolly Bugger
            saddle hackle
Flash: Pearl Krystal Flash
Tail: Black strung marabou

Note: This classic works throughout the year. I like to fish the conehead version the best for the added weight and jigging motion it provides when retrieved. Remember the Woolly Bugger is an impressionistic fly pattern and represents a variety of food groups including baitfish, leeches, and cranefly larvae, depending on the size and color you are fishing. You can add rubber legs, flash, and any number of changes to your Woolly Buggers and find good success. Carry Woolly Buggers in a variety of colors including olive, black, white, and brown.

Leadeye Bighorn Bugger

Hook: #4-8 Daiichi 2220
Thread: Black 6/0 Uni
Body: Brown chenille
Rib: Copper Flashabou
Hackle: Grizzly rooster saddle
            hackle
Eyes: Gold MFC brass dumbbell
            eyes
Legs: Yellow MFC Centipede
            Legs
Rib: Copper wire
Tail: Brown and yellow
            marabou blood quill
Underbody: Lead wire

Note: Brown and yellow has been a classic fall color combination on the Bighorn for years now. The incorporation of lead eyes gets this fly down quickly. This is a staple fly pattern for aggressive browns in the fall.

Coffey's Sparkle Minnow

Hook:	#2-4 Dai-Riki 710
Bead:	Black nickel conehead
Weight:	.030-inch-diameter lead wire
Thread:	Black 3/0 Uni
Tail:	White, olive/brown, and medium olive marabou
Tail Flash:	Copper Krystal Flash
Body:	Gold Ice Dub brush
Underbody:	Pearl Ice Dub brush
Back:	Black Sharpie

Note: Flashy streamers work really well on rivers throughout the West, and this is the king of flashy streamers. I like to use this as the lead fly of a double streamer rig, with a drabber fly in tow. It comes in several color combinations; JJ Special and Sculpin colors seem to work the best. You can also purchase an articulated version that works well in off-color water.

McKnight's Home Invader

Hook:	#2-8 Tiemco 700
Thread:	Burnt orange 140-denier UTC
Eyes:	Painted dumbbell eyes
Body:	Brown and tan marabou, natural red fox
Hackle:	Olive grizzly saddle
Flash:	Copper Flashabou, black pearl Krystal Flash

Note: This is just one of many effective streamers from Livingston-based fishing guide Doug McKnight. The Home Invader accounts for many large trout each year because of the incredible movement and great silhouette it has in the water. The contrasting color tones and variety of natural materials are the other keys to its effectiveness. Olive grizzly, white, and tan are all effective.

Delektable Screamer

Hook:	#4 Dai-Riki 710
Thread:	Black 3/0 Uni
Bead:	Gold 5.5 mm brass cone
Flash:	Gold Holographic tinsel
Body:	Silver Ice Dub
Wing:	Yellow and red barred marabou
Underwing:	Grizzly saddle hackle
Hackle:	Grizzly hackle
Tail:	White marabou

Note: Dan Delekta's Screamer solicits violent strikes. It comes in both single and articulated versions. I really like to work this fly fast through the water when fish are on the chase. My go-to color combination is black and olive; the natural materials in combination with the flashy body make this fly effective in just about any light condition. Yellow/brown and badger are also effective.

Galloup's Peanut Envy

Back Hook:	#6 Daiichi 1750
Thread:	Black GSP 200
Tail:	Black marabou
Body:	Black Ice Dub
Hackle:	Black strung rooster saddle
Rib:	Copper UTC wire
Wing:	Black Woolly Bugger marabou
Legs:	Black/red flake Crazy Legs
Flash:	Red Krystal Flash
Front Hook:	#6 Daiichi 1750
Head:	Black nickel cone (large)
Collar:	Black Ice Dub

Note: In the words of my friend Kelly Galloup: "This fly hunts." This articulated fly has a slim profile yet incredible movement in the water. I like to fish this pattern in white, during the winter and spring season. White and olive are my two favorite colors, with black also effective, in size 4 and 6.

Barr's Meat Whistle

Hook:	#1/0-1 Gamakatsu 90-degree jig
Cone:	Copper tungsten cone (large)
Thread:	Rusty brown 140-denier UTC
Rib:	Copper brown UTC Ultra Wire (Brassie)
Body:	Copper Sparkle Braid
Wing:	Rusty brown rabbit strip
Legs:	Pumpkin barred Sili Legs
Flash:	Copper Flashabou
Collar:	Brown marabou

Note: The combination of the rabbit strip, rubber legs, and flash make this an effective imitation for small baitfish and leeches. In addition to providing great movement in the water, the jig-style hook rides up and doesn't get snagged on the bottom when fishing shallow riffles or using a heavy sink tip. Black, crawdad (brown), and white are all effective colors.

Bonefish Clouser

Hook:	#2-6 Tiemco 800
Thread:	Tan 210-denier UTC
Eyes:	Yellow-painted lead eyes
Body:	Yellow, cream, and white Craft Fur
Flash:	Root beer Krystal Flash
Legs:	Tan/black Centipede Legs
Beard:	Tan brown barred rabbit

Note: This fly is equally at home on the flats as it is on the Bighorn River. I started fishing saltwater patterns such as the Crazy Charlie and many others to imitate whitefish minnows. The color combination is just right for this river, and the rubber legs add that much more appeal. The heavy eyes keep the fly down and the saltwater hook is great for setting the hook on big fish.

Aram's Lil Kim

Hook:	#4-8 Tiemco 9395
Thread:	Black GSP 75-denier UTC
Flash:	Gold Flashabou and midge flash
Tail:	Olive brown marabou blood quill
Abdomen:	Red Saltwater Flashabou
Wing:	Olive brown marabou blood quills
Overwing:	Black/olive midge flash
Rib:	Gold UV Polar Chenille
Throat:	Red midge flash
Cheeks:	Pearl Flashabou
Collar:	Olive schlappen
Head:	Gold cone

Note: This streamer was created by Aram Aykanian. The combination of olive and gold flash in this fly is highly effective. This is one of my go-to streamers during the summer and on bright days because of its natural coloration and lifelike movement.

Circus Peanut

Hook:	#4 Tiemco 5263
Thread:	Danville 210 and 6/0 Uni, color to match body
Eyes:	Red-painted lead eyes
Weedguard:	25-pound mono
Tail:	Olive marabou
Flash:	Pearl Flashabou
Body:	Olive Crystal Chenille
Hackle:	Black schlappen
Legs:	Olive/green/pea Sili Legs

Note: Russ Maddin's Circus Peanut is a big-fish-catching machine and has inspired many of the great big-fish streamers available today. It incorporates all the key characteristics that attract trout—flash, rubber legs, movement, and a big silhouette. Black, olive, and white are all effective colors.

JR's Conehead Streamer

Hook:	#4-8 Dai-Riki 710
Head:	Silver 4.8 mm brass cone
Thread:	White 6/0 Uni
Rabbit:	Olive brown barred rabbit strips
Hackle:	White Metz soft-hackle
Body:	Pearl Ice Dub, silver wire
Eyes:	Gold ¼ Hologram Dome Eyes

Note: John Rohmer's streamer works well on every trout water I have ever fished. It is not usually responsible for catching the largest trout of the day, but it is great for producing an excellent number of hook-ups. All the color combinations of this fly are effective, such as tan, gray, black, and olive. Olive/white is especially effective on the Bighorn.

AQUATIC INSECTS

Midges

As with every tailwater, midges are extremely plentiful on the Bighorn River. In the winter and early spring, while water temperatures are still too cold for mayfly hatches, midges are the predominant insect hatch and the trout's main food supply. The abundance of larvae and pupae in the Bighorn makes it easy for the trout to feed while expending little energy when their metabolism is at its lowest point.

Good midge fishing starts in February and often lasts well into May. As water temperatures warm up from February to May, the window each day in which midge emergences occur will widen. Nymph fishing with larvae and pupae imitations can be good at any time of the day. Typically surface action will start at 10 a.m. with single adults and emergers. Fishing midge clusters will start getting good in the early afternoon. An overlooked time in the spring during midge emergences is the last hour before dark. In February you may only get a two-hour window of good surface action, whereas in April fishing can be good all day. Good fishing with adult midge clusters only occurs once the hatches become dense enough. Midge fishing is at its best on the upper 3 miles, where these hatches are the most prolific, but midge patterns fish well all the way down to Bighorn Access.

Midges go through a complete metamorphosis, which includes a larva, pupa, and adult stage. While midge larvae are effective fished along the bottom, midge pupae ascending to the surface are most vulnerable to the trout. Because of cold water and their minute size, it takes a long time for them to reach the surface. Once they almost reach the surface, the surface film further impedes the pupae. They collect here and trout gorge on these easy pickings.

Trout key in on midge pupae as they ascend to the surface during a hatch. JIM SCHOLLMEYER

A midge pupa imitation fished on a greased leader or trailed behind a midge adult dry fly is deadly during the midge hatch. Having a stable of fly patterns that sit just below or flush to the film is important for success in the spring. A standard black midge pupa, dropped a short distance off of a midge cluster, or a CDC Transitional Midge are two of the best patterns for targeting these fish feeding in the surface film. Anglers sometimes find this kind of fishing frustrating, because these imitations are nearly impossible to see, but using hi-vis point flies makes it easy to follow the pair. When fishing any small dry, take the time to apply floatant if you can't see your fly.

Throughout the winter and early spring, midge adults will be airborne during the warmest part of the day. Look for fish to key in on single midge adults in the late morning and focus on mating clusters in the afternoons and evenings. A standard Griffith's Gnat or Twilight Midge are perfect representations of the natural clusters, which can get so large that you will want to carry imitations all the way up to a size 14.

As we move further into spring and the water begins to warm, look for Blue-Winged Olives (*Baetis*) to hatch simultaneously with midges. While the gray-winged BWOs, with their sailboat silhouette, will be easily noticed on the surface of the water, the fish may well be eating midge adults or clusters. Fishing a BWO dry up front with a midge cluster trailed 16 to 18 inches behind it is a great way to approach rising fish at this time of the year.

Success with fishing midges below the surface comes down to selecting an imitation that is the right size and color. Midges are available in a wide variety of colors and sizes throughout the year. Larvae and pupae may be present in black, brown, olive, cream, and red, and it is important to carry variations of each. Bighorn trout readily key in on a certain color midge—be it hourly, daily, or weekly. In the spring, I use a stomach pump to determine the color larvae or pupae the fish are keying in on. You will often get midge larvae from a trout's digestive tract that are still moving. You should pay attention to the size and color of these especially.

As an angler, it is also crucial to be able to differentiate a midge larva from a midge pupa. The larvae simply look like tiny, segmented, tube-like worms. When these larvae transform into pupae, they grow clear, or white, wing buds that are easily identified by anglers. Being able to recognize this will allow you to correctly identify the naturals you have collected and select a proper imitation from your fly box.

Zebra Midge

Hook:	#18-24 Dai-Riki 135
Bead:	Peacock metallic Killer Caddis (small)
Thread:	Black 8/0 Uni
Rib:	Silver wire (small)

Note: A black Zebra Midge (also good in cream, red, and olive) is a viable fly choice every day on the Bighorn. Trout eat midge larvae year-round, predominantly in the late winter and spring seasons. I prefer to tie these with silver tungsten or peacock glass beads. I often fish the tungsten version as a dropper off a dry fly.

Yong Midge

Hook:	#18-20 Daiichi 1110
Thread:	Black 8/0 Uni
Body:	Summer brown Coats and Clark (ART210 A354A)
Head:	Tying thread and flat pearl tinsel (small)

Note: This San Juan River larva pattern's segmented body created by the sewing thread is the key to its effectiveness. On the Bighorn, versions tied with and without flash in brown, cream, and olive are effective.

Cream Midge

Hook: #18-20 Daiichi 1130
Thread: Cream 6/0 Danville
Body: Tying thread
Rib: Gold UTC Wire (small)

Note: When trout key in on cream midges, this pattern by Bighorn River guide David Dill is the one to tie on. I really like the contrasting black head. Use your stomach pump and seine to determine when cream midges are available to the trout. When they are present, the fish key in on them readily.

Root Beer Midge

Hook: #16-20 Dai-Riki 075
Thread: Black 8/0 Uni
Body: Rust Wapsi Stretch Tubing
Thorax: Adams gray Superfine
Wing: White Antron yarn

Note: In the Bighorn, root beer-colored midge pupae are common. The transparent body material used for the abdomen and the synthetic wing case perfectly imitate an emerging midge pupa. This is the midge pupa that we sell the most of in the shop each spring.

Red Midge Larva

Hook: #12-20 Daiichi 1130
Thread: Red 8/0 Uni
Body: Red Wapsi Stretch Tubing

Note: So simple, yet so effective—trout will feed on red midge larvae all spring. This fly is almost as popular with Bighorn anglers as the black Zebra Midge. This is one of the first patterns I try when the fish are being picky any time of the year.

Black Beauty Emerger

Hook: #18-22 Daiichi 1130
Thread: Black 8/0 Uni
Tail: Gray Antron yarn
Body: Black 8/0 Uni
Rib: Silver Ultra Wire
Wing: White Antron yarn
Head: Adams gray Superfine

Note: I fish this pattern to match midge pupae ascending to the surface. I will often stop my fly mid-drift and let it slowly swing up to the surface to draw a strike.

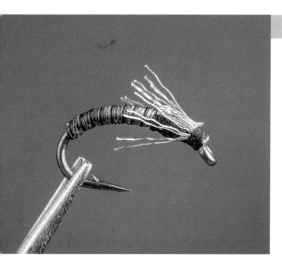

Juju Midge

Hook:	#18-20 Dai-Riki 135
Thread:	Black 8/0 Uni
Body:	Black and olive Superhair/Slinky Fibre
Wing Case:	White Fluoro Fibre

Note: Charlie Craven's midge pupa is a must-have on any trout river and works especially well on the Bighorn. I like to fish this in olive/black and all-black. The body is formed from two strands of black Superhair/Slinky Fibre and one strand of olive Superhair/Slinky Fibre.

Tungteaser

Hook:	#18-20 Dai-Riki 135
Bead:	Silver $5/64$" tungsten
Thread:	Black 8/0 Uni
Tail/Wing:	Black Antron yarn
Rib:	Small silver wire
Body:	Black $1/8$" Scud Back

Note: The Tungteaser is an impressionistic fly that works well throughout the entire year. The tungsten bead allows this fly to sink quickly. While it primarily imitates a midge, it works really well as a Trico nymph or black caddis pupa imitation.

CDC Transitional Midge

Hook:	#18-22 Daiichi 1100
Tail:	Grizzly saddle hackle tips
Thread:	Gray 8/0 Uni
Body:	Adams gray Superfine
Wing:	Natural dun CDC

Note: This low-riding, emerging surface midge by René Harrop has been effective everywhere I fish it. This is my go-to midge pattern in technical midge fishing situations when fish are feeding in the surface film, often indicated when you only see the trout's tail break the surface.

Smokejumper

Hook:	#18-20 Daiichi 1130
Wing:	Black premium CDC
Body:	Black 8/0 Uni
Thorax:	Peacock

Note: In gray and black, this is one of the most popular emerging midge patterns on the Bighorn. The highly visible CDC wing sits high while the body hangs just below the surface, perfectly imitating the insect breaking the water's surface tension.

Student CDC Emerger

Hook:	#18-22 Daiichi 1100
Tail:	Light brown Antron yarn
Thread:	Gray 8/0 Uni
Body:	Peacock quill
Thorax:	Adams gray Superfine
Wing:	Natural dun CDC

Note: Colorado tier David Student's pattern is deadly when midges are emerging. This fly sits in the surface film and works great on fish feeding in or just below the surface film. It is hard to see on the water and should be fished behind a larger dry fly.

Parachute Adams

Hook:	#18-24 Daiichi 1100
Thread:	Black 8/0 Uni
Body:	Adams gray Superfine
Hackle:	Brown and grizzly hackle
Wing:	Black Antron yarn

Note: Probably the best adult midge imitation there is. I carry them with white, black, and pink posts so I am ready to fish during any light conditions. To overcome glare on the water during overcast days, I like the black post, and early or late in the day, I like the pink post.

Twilight Midge

Hook:	#18-22 Daiichi 1100
Thread:	Black 8/0 Uni
Body:	Peacock herl
Hackle:	Grizzly
Post:	Fluorescent orange Antron

Note: The Twilight Midge is a great cluster imitation, similar to a Griffith's Gnat in that it has a peacock body and grizzly hackle, though the hackle is wrapped around a fluorescent post instead of through the body. This fly is a great indicator in a two-fly dry-fly rig.

Griffith's Gnat

Hook:	#14-20 Daiichi 1100
Thread:	Black 8/0 Uni
Body:	Peacock herl
Hackle:	Grizzly

Note: The Griffith's Gnat is an essential midge cluster imitation. At times I like to trim the hackle on the bottom, so the fly sits flush on the water.

Renegade

Hook:	#18-20 Daiichi 1100
Thread:	Black 8/0 Uni
Body:	Peacock herl
Hackle:	Brown and white
Tag:	Gold tinsel

Note: This overlooked classic is a great cluster and dead midge imitation and is probably as effective as any other pattern when midges are present. It works any time during the year.

Midge Life Cycle Patterns

Larvae/Pupae

Zebra Midge (#18-22; black, red, cream, olive)
Yong Midge (#18-20; brown, cream)
Red Midge Larva (#12-20)
Root Beer Midge (#16-20)
Juju Midge (#18-20; olive, black)
Jailbird Midge (#18-20; black, cream, red)

Emergers

Black Beauty Emerger (#18-20)
Birschell's Hatching Midge (#18-20; gray, cream)
CDC Transitional Midge (#18-20)

Adults

Harrop Hanging Midge (#18-22; black, gray)
Parachute Adams (#18-22)
Zelon Midge (#18-22; gray, black, cream)

Clusters

Griffith's Gnat (#16-22)
Twilight Midge (#16-22)
Renegade (#18-20)

MAYFLIES

Mayflies go through incomplete metamorphosis (no pupal stage). At the least, you should carry a few nymph, dun, and spinner patterns for each hatch. However, a thorough fly box for the river should contain standard nymphs, emerging nymphs, floating nymphs, cripples, stillborn emergers, half-in/half-out surface emergers, standard duns, hi-vis duns, low-floating duns, spinners, and egg-laying spinners. You will also want to carry these patterns in multiple sizes and color variations to match the hatch as best as possible.

Blue-Winged Olives

Blue-Winged Olives, frequently referred to as *Baetis* or BWOs, are the first significant mayfly hatch of the season, and their arrival is highly anticipated by anglers and the trout each year. Unlike other mayflies, *Baetis* produce several broods throughout the year. Spring *Baetis* hatch predominantly in March, April, and May. I have seen the spring hatch last continuously into August, typically during years when water temperatures are colder than normal. The spring *Baetis* emerge in size 16 to 18 and hatch in abundance. The body color of the Blue-Winged Olives is directly correlated with the amount of sunlight present when the hatch occurs. This is why adults that hatch in March will be darker than adults that hatch in May or June. I have seen *Baetis* present in a wide variety of colors including olive brown, olive gray, and even a light yellowish olive. I tie all my favorite BWO patterns in each color.

The most significant factor affecting the BWO emergence each spring is water temperature. I have seen Blue-Winged Olives hatch on the lower river down near Two Leggins Access a good two weeks before seeing any on the upper river. The magic temperature for this hatch seems to be right around 43 degrees, which is typically reached in the afternoon, during the warmest part of the day. For this reason, carrying a thermometer in your vest or pack is a good idea.

Bighorn trout love slender-bodied Blue-Winged Olive nymphs, which are of the most importance to the angler during the spring.
JIM SCHOLLMEYER

While we all enjoy fishing to rising trout on the surface, the nymphs and emerging nymphs offer tremendous opportunity to the angler. Rainbow and brown trout thrive and quickly fatten up each spring by gorging on *Baetis* nymphs dislodged from the river bottom and ascending to the surface. Nymphs dead-drifted near the bottom are always effective.

When the nymph's abdomen and wing case become almost black in color, it is ready to emerge. Once the water temperature warms each day, these dark nymphs will begin to emerge to the surface. Classified as swimmers, *Baetis* nymphs emerge rapidly to the surface and are taken readily by trout. The Wonder Nymph, created by longtime Bighorn River guide Brad Downey, is effective at imitating these emerging nymphs.

A great way to induce a strike when *Baetis* nymphs are emerging is by stopping your flies mid-drift and allowing them to rise to the surface. On countless occasions I have had clients begin to strip their line in to recast and a fish takes their fly. Another technique that works well is to give your flies a few slow but deliberate strips right before your drift is about to drag out below you. This will cause viscous strikes by feeding trout.

Once the emerging mayflies have reached the surface film, or are drifting on the surface as duns, trout switch to adults on the surface. BWO duns can range in size from 16 to 22 throughout the year, with duns largest at the start of the yearly emergence. While a drag-free presentation

While small in size, *Pseudocloeon* can emerge in great abundance during the late summer and fall seasons. While the average angler may feel overwhelmed at first by the *Pseudocloeon* emergence, patience and persistence will always lead to success. Dry-fly aficionados can rely on this emergence yearly to provide spectacular fall dry-fly fishing.

and accurate drift are always required, fish are not nearly as selective when it comes to fishing this hatch early in the spring. Large pods of surface feeders allow the angler to approach relatively close. The trout seem to let their guards down during the climax of the Blue-Winged Olive emergence. I know a hatch of BWOs is at its best when the entire surface of the river is blanketed in insects and the geese and swallows are feeding as ferociously as the trout!

While Bighorn trout will take high-riding adult imitations regularly, stealthier patterns that sit lower in the surface film are often more effective. When mayflies hatch, they break out of their nymphal shucks in the surface film and then need to dry their wings before they can leave the surface of the water. At this time the insect is helpless and in its most vulnerable state to the trout. Insects that are half in and half out of their nymphal shuck are represented by your typical emerger pattern. A BWO dun that is trapped in a partially opened shuck, or that has not been able to dry its wings—either because it is too cold or too wet to do so—and cannot leave the surface of the water is called a cripple. The colder and wetter the conditions, the longer it takes for a mayfly to fully emerge and take flight. Bighorn trout have been conditioned to take advantage of this stage of the emergence and can feed on this stage exclusively at any given time. Surface and crippled emerger patterns should be a must in every angler's fly box for the Blue-Winged Olive hatch.

While the fall Blue-Winged Olives carry the same characteristics as the spring *Baetis* hatch, they are not found in as great abundance as in the spring. You should be prepared to see fall *Baetis* throughout October and November in size 18 and 20. It is the *Pseudocloeon* in the fall that are most prevalent, and they should have your greatest focus when looking for surface action in the fall.

Pseudos were once their own genus (*Pseudocleons*) but have recently been lumped in with the *Baetis* genus. Pseudos are now commonly referred to as Tiny Blue-Winged Olives. On the Bighorn, many anglers and guides still refer to them as Pseudos. For the avid dry-fly angler, the Pseudo can create some terrific technical dry-fly fishing, displaying similar characteristics to those of Blue-Winged Olives. This hatch occurs on overcast afternoons in September and October. Pseudos can emerge in amazing abundance, to the point where they will blanket the surface and you can scoop them up by the handfuls where they collect along the river's edge. An exacting presentation and accurate cast, with just the right imitation, is a must when the fish are feeding on them. For anglers not willing to tempt their fate with a dry fly, Bighorn trout readily take these tiny nymphs as they emerge off the river bottom. A Skinny Bill, tiny Pheasant Tail, or Pseudo Wonder Nymph are great nymph imitations.

Black Quill

Hook:	#18-20 Dai-Riki 070
Thread:	Black 8/0 Uni
Tail:	Natural pheasant tail
Rib:	Gold UTC (small)
Abdomen:	Tying thread
Thorax:	Peacock herl
Wing Case:	Mylar tinsel

Note: Behind the Ray Charles, this is the most effective nymph pattern on the river. It imitates Blue-Winged Olives, Tricos, and midge pupae well. General nymphs such as this (with a peacock glass bead and also without) can catch trout every day of the year. The Black Quill can also be tied using cream and olive thread to match the immature Pseudo and *Baetis* nymphs.

Flashback Pheasant Tail

Hook:	#16-22 Dai-Riki 075
Tail/Body:	Natural pheasant tail
Rib:	Amber UTC Wire (small)
Thread:	Brown 8/0 Uni
Thorax:	Peacock
Wing Case:	Mylar tinsel

Note: This classic imitates every mayfly nymph in the river and even caddis pupae. With and without beads, fish it in sizes 18 to 20 in the spring and in the summer for size 20 to 22 Pseudos.

JR's Flashback Emerger

Hook:	#18-22 Dai-Riki 075
Thread:	Gray 6/0 Danville
Tail:	Natural pheasant tail
Rib:	Gold wire (fine)
Abdomen:	Gray 6/0 Danville
Thorax:	Adams gray Superfine
Wing Case:	Mylar tinsel
Bead:	Pearl glass bead

Note: This fly by North Platte angler John Robitaille is a great emerging nymph pattern when Blue-Winged Olives or Pseudos are emerging. The gray body offers the fish a different look than many other patterns, and the glass bead looks like the gas bubble of an ascending mayfly nymph.

Downey's Wonder Nymph

Hook:	#16-20 Dai-Riki 075
Thread:	Black 8/0 Uni
Thorax:	Adams gray Hareline Dubbin
Body:	Split-black micro tubing or Scud Back
Tail:	Hungarian partridge
Wing:	Grizzly hackle
Overwing:	Black holographic tinsel (optional)

Note: In olive and black, this pattern created by longtime Bighorn River guide Brad Downey is one of the most consistent emerging BWO nymph imitations every year. I use the black version right before and during the hatch to imitate mature nymphs ascending to the surface. This is a pattern I almost always let swing out at the end of the drift, then retrieve back with small strips.

Juju Baetis

Hook:	#16-20 Dai-Riki 135
Thread:	Black 8/0
Tail:	Hungarian partridge
Body:	Black Supreme Hair
Wing Case:	Pearl tinsel
Wing:	Fluorofibre

Note: This Blue-Winged Olive nymph pattern, created by Colorado-based tier Charlie Craven, is a deadly nymph pattern. The hard, clear coating on the abdomen, slim profile, and just the right amount of flash on the wing case make this pattern irresistible to trout.

Bighorn Emerging Baetis

Hook:	#16-20 Dai-Riki 060
Bead:	Gunmetal Killer Caddis (midge)
Thread:	Black 6/0 Uni
Body:	Adams gray Superfine
Rib:	Silver copper (small)
Tail:	Natural Hungarian partridge
Wing:	Premium black CDC

Note: This pattern, created by Bighorn River guide David Palmer, has all the right characteristics that perfectly represent an emerging Blue-Winged Olive nymph. The gunmetal bead and CDC wing are the key elements to its effectiveness. I fish this fly in gray in sizes 18 and 20 for the spring BWOs and tie it in cream in sizes 20 and 22 to imitate the *Pseudocloeon*.

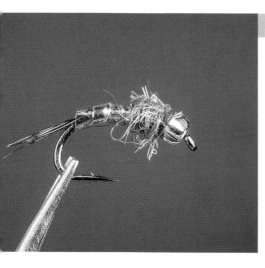

Egan's Rainbow Warrior

Hook:	#16-20 Dai-Riki 135
Thread:	Fire orange 8/0 Uni
Bead:	Crystal pearl Killer Caddis (midge)
Body:	Pearl tinsel, flat (medium)
Thorax:	Rainbow Sow Scud
Tail:	Natural pheasant tail feathers

Note: This great attractor nymph imitates just about every mayfly nymph, especially BWO nymphs. I fish most often this fly in the spring during off-color water conditions.

Mercer's Micro Mayfly

Hook:	#16-22 Dai-Riki 075
Bead:	Gold 2.4 mm brass
Thread:	Dark brown 8/0 Uni
Head:	Chocolate brown Hareline Dubbin
Wing Case:	Pearl tinsel and 5-minute epoxy
Body:	Peacock quill
Tail:	Olive-dyed pheasant tail

Note: This is my favorite fly to use as a nymph in a dry-dropper rig when *Pseudocloeon* are present. The slim body and heavy bead are the keys to its effectiveness.

CDC RS-2

Hook:	#18-22 Dai-Riki 075
Thread:	Gray 8/0 Uni
Body:	Adams gray Superfine
Wing:	Natural dun or black CDC
Wire:	Copper UTC (small)
Tail:	Natural Hungarian partridge

Note: This is one of the most versatile flies you will find for fishing the Bighorn River when small mayflies are emerging. You can fish it under an indicator as an emerging nymph or behind a dry fly in the surface film. Cream, olive, and gray are the best colors.

CDC Biot Dun

Hook:	#18-22 Daiichi 1100
Thread:	Olive 8/0 Uni
Tail:	Light dun CDC fibers and light dun hackle fibers
Abdomen:	Turkey biot
Thorax:	Olive gray Superfine
Wing/Legs:	Natural dun CDC feathers

Note: This René Harrop–designed mayfly imitation has a great-looking profile when it rides on the surface. It works equally well for both Blue-Winged Olives and Pseudos.

The Student

Hook:	#18-22 Daiichi 1100
Thread:	Olive dun 8/0 Uni
Tail/Wing:	Natural dun Trouthunter CDC

Note: This pattern created by longtime Montana guide Frank Johnson has been the go-to small mayfly dry for picky fish. This is the fly you need for those fish lazily sipping dry flies in the flat water. The sparse tie of this fly is the key to its success. Keep it floating with desiccant powder and you will be into fish all day.

CDC Sparkle Dun

Hook:	#16-20 Daiichi 1100
Thread:	Olive dun 8/0 Uni
Wing:	Natural dark dun CDC
Body:	Adams gray Superfine
Tail:	Dark brown Antron yarn

Note: This is my go-to imitation for Blue-Winged Olives or any mayfly. It perfectly imitates an emerging BWO dun. The shuck used for the tail sits low in the water and the CDC wing rides high in the air, making this fly effective and easy to see. I fish this fly with an olive (early spring) or gray body depending on the time of year.

Crippled Thor

Hook:	#16-20 Daiichi 1100
Thread:	Olive dun 8/0 Uni
Tail:	Hungarian partridge
Rib:	Gold UTC (small)
Wing:	Natural dun CDC
Abdomen:	Thread

Note: The Crippled Thor created by longtime Bighorn angler Roger "Thor" Hiel has been the go-to BWO pattern for years. The CDC wing rides high on the water and the body sits low in the film. You can tie this to represent a Pale Morning Dun, and it will work equally well.

Harrop CDC Paraspinner

Hook:	#16-20 Daiichi 1100
Thread:	Olive dun 8/0 Uni
Body:	Olive turkey biot
Wing:	White CDC
Thorax:	BWO Superfine
Tail:	Light speckled Coq de Leon
Hackle:	Grizzly (oversized)

Note: In my opinion, there is no deadlier pattern for imitating mayfly spinners. The long abdomen, split tails, and sparse hackle that sits flush with the surface make this fly a killer. The CDC post keeps this fly visible to the angler as well. This fly is especially effective in the flats where trout congregate to feed on spinners. You should carry these in colors to imitate BWOs, PMDs, and Tricos, and in rusty to cover just about any mayfly emergence.

BWO Fly Box

Nymphs

Wonder Nymph (#18-20; olive, black)
Juju Baetis (#18-20; black)
Rainbow Warrior (#16-20)
Killer Mayfly (#18-22; black, olive)
Flashback Pheasant Tail (#16-22)
Quill Nymph (#18-20; black, cream, olive)
JR's Flashback Emerger (#18-20)

Emergers

Smokejumper (#18-20; olive, gray)
Sipper Emerger (#18-20; olive, gray)
Crippled Thor (#18-20)
CDC RS-2 (#18-20; gray, olive, cream)
Bighorn Emerging Baetis (#18-20)

Duns/Spinners

The Student (#18-22)
CDC Sparkle Dun (#16-20; gray, olive,
   olive/brown)
CDC Biot Dun (#18-22; olive, olive/gray)
Parachute Adams (#18-22; gray, olive)
Tailwater Dun (#18-20)
CDC Paraspinner (#18-22; olive, rusty)
Hi-Vis CDC Paraspinner (#18-20)

Pale Morning Dun

The Pale Morning Dun (PMD) hatch will test your skills unlike any other mayfly hatch in the Rocky Mountain West. PMD hatches can occur on the Bighorn River in June, July, and August. There are two species of PMDs that hatch on the Bighorn: the larger *infrequens* and the smaller *inermis*. Depending on the species, PMDs hatch in sizes 14 to 18. Their body color ranges anywhere from a pale yellow to cream or even a creamy orange or sulphur color. The size and color of this mayfly depends on water temperature, amount of sunlight, and how far along the hatch is within their seasonal emergence. Water temperatures in the mid-50s and cloudy days bring out the best Pale Morning Dun emergences, which typically occur between 11 a.m. and 3 p.m.

Bighorn trout readily key in on Pale Morning Dun nymphs. Once the wing case darkens, these nymphs lazily ascend to the surface in fast water riffles throughout the Bighorn. The sheer abundance and lackadaisical nature of these nymphs allow trout to easily intercept them throughout the water column. As the nymph is reaching the surface to emerge, the wing case splits open and a pronounced band of yellow shows through the "split" in the case. This stage of the emergence, which trout gorge on, is what the highly effective Split Case PMD nymph imitates so well.

The Pale Morning Dun is a delicate insect whose success at emerging into an adult depends on several environmental variables such as air temperature, light conditions, and moisture content. For this reason, Pale Morning Duns are probably more susceptible to predation during the emerger stage than any other aquatic insect. Most often your success as an angler while matching the PMD hatch will depend on how well you imitate the emerger stage. Anglers should carry a wide variety of emerger patterns that represent the partially hatched adult, half in and half out of the nymphal shuck, along with a variety of crippled and stillborn patterns to catch the larger feeding fish.

While fishing emergers in the surface film will often bring you the most success, during certain stages of the hatch adult imitations can be the ticket. If there is one imitation that I feel most confident about fishing during this hatch, it is the CDC Sparkle Dun. This pattern works well at imitating fully emerged adults, yet sits low in the water and offers a tailing material that imitates a shuck that trout key in on.

There may be no finer dry-fly experience on the Bighorn than that of a Pale Morning Dun spinner fall. These spinner falls typically occur in the late morning and can bring the water to a boil with rising trout. Novice anglers overlook this stage of the emergence. It does not take many spinners to be present for the trout to really key in on them. Harrop's CDC Paraspinner and the Rusty Spinner are effective for imitating this stage.

Unfortunately the PMD hatch does not occur each year; this is especially true for the upper 3 river miles, where water temperatures are the coldest. If the hatch doesn't occur river-wide on a given year, you can typically find it in specific runs from Three Mile Access to Bighorn Access or throughout the lower river where water temperatures are warmer.

The sight of Pale Morning Duns floating on the surface of the Bighorn is one of the most exciting experiences you can have in fly fishing.
JIM SCHOLLMEYER

Split Case PMD

Hook:	#16-20 Dai-Riki 060
Thread:	Dark brown 8/0 Uni
Tail:	Tan mallard flank
Rib:	6X monofilament
Body:	Chocolate brown Hareline Dubbin
Wing:	Yellow foam cut small with brown goose biots pulled around sides
Legs:	Tan mallard flank (short)

Note: The key to this pattern is the yellow spot in the "split" wing case. This is a trigger that trout respond to extremely well as the nymphs ascend to the surface. Carry this must-have pattern with and without a tungsten bead, which works well in a dry-dropper rig.

Soft-Hackle Hare's Ear

Hook:	#14-18 Dai-Riki 070
Thread:	Tan 8/0 Uni
Rib:	Gold tinsel
Body:	Natural hare's mask
Hackle:	Hungarian partridge

Note: This classic fly pattern is still effective. Fish it under an indicator, swing it through a riffle, or hand twist it through a pod of risers to imitate an emerging nymph.

Quigley Half Dun

Hook:	#14-18 Daiichi 1100
Thread:	Light cahill 8/0 Uni
Tail:	Micro Krystal Flash and natural fur tips
Wing:	Gray poly yarn
Hackle:	Cream rooster saddle
Thorax:	PMD yellow Superfine

Note: This brilliant creation, by the late Bob Quigley, is the answer to breaking the PMD hatch code. This pattern can imitate a PMD cripple, emerger, or spinner effectively. It is one of those patterns that will leave you guessing when you see it in a fly bin, but will bring you back for more once you've fished it.

Sipper Emerger

Hook:	#16-20 Daiichi 1140
Thread:	Light cahill 8/0 Uni
Abdomen:	PMD turkey biot
Underwing:	Natural dun Trouthunter CDC
Wing:	Deer hair
Head:	PMD yellow Superfine

Note: I created this pattern to imitate an emerging mayfly half in and half out of the surface film. It is highly effective when fish are feeding in the surface film. The deer-hair/CDC wing is easy to see.

PMD Fly Box

Nymphs

Mercer's Poxyback PMD (#16-18)
Split Case PMD (#16-20)
Wonder Nymph PMD (#16-18)

Emergers

Quigley Half Dun (#16-18)
Sipper Emerger (#14-18)
Brook's Sprout Emerger (#14-16)

Duns/Spinners

Crippled Thor (#14-18)
Orange Sulphur Parachute (#14-16)
CDC Sparkle Dun (#14-18; cream)
Harrop Paraspinner (#14-18; PMD yellow, rusty)
Hi-Vis CDC Paraspinner (#14-16)

Trico

Tricos are an intimidating hatch for some anglers to match, but these size 18 to 22 mayflies turn Bighorn trout into voracious feeders. I don't know of another water body where the Trico emergence lasts as long as it does on the Bighorn. I have seen the duns hatch as early as July and as late as November. The bulk of the hatch comes off from August through October and becomes the trout's main focus in the morning and early afternoons.

The Trico hatch depends on air temperature and weather. The duns hatch the best on cloudy, overcast days in both early morning and late evening, although hatches will still occur on bright, sunny days, especially during the height of the hatch. Fish key in on the duns from sun-up until about 9 a.m. each morning. Many people overlook the evening Trico emergence. There have been many nights, when we were collecting our rentals boats at Bighorn Access, that we were covered by emerging duns. On cooler days in the fall, these emerging duns become important because spinner falls won't always take place.

Trico spinner falls occur best on warm sunny days. Spinners typically begin to fall around 10 a.m. and, during the best occurrences, last into the early afternoon. Spinner falls occur after the adults have completed their mating cycle. When completed, the males fall to the water to die and the females go to the water to lay their eggs, then die. These spent spinners are easy prey for the trout because of the sheer volume of them that all fall to the water at the same time, sometimes blanketing every square inch of the water's surface, which can make for some difficult fishing because of all the naturals competing with your fly.

Anglers should focus their attention on fishing these spinner falls. But also be prepared to fish the duns in the morning. Fishing a spinner pattern trailed behind a more visible dun pattern is often your best course of

Tricos are one of the most reliable summer hatches on the Bighorn, and the trout key in on the spinners readily.
JIM SCHOLLMEYER

action once the hatch has begun. Fishing a Purple Haze or CDC Thorax Dun, with a generic spinner trailed off the back, while the duns are emerging is a good place to start. Once the spinners start moving closer to the water's surface and I get a few takes on the spinner, I switch over to a double Trico spinner rig that consists of a highly visible spinner imitation, such as the Hi-Vis CDC Paraspinner, on top with a traditional biot spinner or Harrop Paraspinner trailed behind.

Being able to locate your fly in relation to a specific fish is critical for success. Fish often feed in tight pods during the hatch, and takes can be subtle and happen quickly. Having a high-visibility point fly is essential to detecting strikes.

Carlson's Purple Haze

Hook:	#18-20 Daiichi 1100
Thread:	Black 6/0 Danville
Body:	Purple Flex Floss
Tail:	Natural brown elk hair
Post:	White calf tail

Note: Why purple is such an effective color is anyone's guess, but it works. This highly visible parachute fly is a great indicator fly to use in combination with a Trico spinner when duns are emerging.

CDC Thorax Dun (Trico)

Hook: #18-22 Daiichi 1100
Thread: Black 8/0 Uni
Body: Turkey biot
Tail: Grizzly saddle hackle
Wing: White CDC

Note: This fly has exactly the right profile needed to fish Trico duns. I believe the biot body and CDC wing are the keys to its effectiveness.

YFG Trico Dun

Hook: #18-22 Daiichi 1100
Thread: Black 8/0 Uni
Body: Thread
Wing: Natural white premium CDC
Thorax: Black Superfine
Tail: Light dun Microfibetts

Note: The slender body on this fly is the key to its effectiveness. The large white wing is easy to see and doesn't spook the fish. This is my favorite dun imitation point fly for when it is hard to see my fly on the water.

Hi-Vis CDC Paraspinner

Hook:	#18-20 Daiichi 1100
Thread:	Rusty brown 8/0 Uni
Tail:	Light dun Microfibetts
Egg Sac:	Yellow Superfine
Body:	Rusty turkey biot
Post:	Fluorescent orange poly yarn
Hackle:	Grizzly saddle hackle

Note: I use this pattern as a point fly during a spinner fall. While it doesn't always get eaten, it is realistic enough to hook fish at the start of the emergence when the fish are a little less picky.

CDC Biot Spinner (Trico)

Hook:	#18-22 Daiichi 1110
Thread:	Black 8/0 Uni
Body:	Rusty turkey biot
Thorax:	Black Superfine
Wing:	White Trouthunter CDC
Tail:	Light dun Microfibetts

Note: This biot-bodied spinner is one of the most realistic spent spinner imitations you can find. Keep the spent CDC dry with desiccant and you will be able to see this fly well. I like to trail this fly behind a Hi-Vis CDC Paraspinner or YFG Trico Dun.

Trico Fly Box

Nymphs
Pheasant Tail (#18-22)
Palmer's Trico Nymph (#18-22)
Tungteaser (#18-20)

Spinners
Biot Spinner (#18-22)
Harrop CDC Paraspinner (#18-22)
Hi-Vis CDC Paraspinner (#18-20)

Adults
Parachute Adams (#18-22)
Carlson's Purple Haze (#18-20)
CDC Thorax Dun (#18-20)

YELLOW SALLY

Yellow Sallies (also called Little Yellow Sallies) are the only stonefly species present on the Bighorn and require well-oxygenated water and a clean gravel bottom. They do especially well following a few years of high water, when the gravel river bottom is free of sediment. The Yellow Sally hatch coincides with the Pale Morning Dun hatch from June through August. The size 12 to 14 adult Sallies are easy to see in the air; their bright yellow bodies and the pronounced red abdomen on the females are dead giveaways of their presence. The trout respond well to both the adults and nymphs throughout the entire river from top to bottom. During some low-water years, this emergence can be limited to the lower river from Bighorn Access to Two Leggins Access.

This is one of the hatches when we tend to fish our imitations blind at the bank, a technique typically reserved for terrestrials. A Yellow PMX with a nymph dropper or with a more realistic imitation can be highly effective. Nymph imitations such as Kyle's Beadhead Yellow Sally and the Tungsten Sallie fished through well-oxygenated riffles are top subsurface producers throughout the hatch. While you will locate fish feeding on Yellow Sallies in pods, blind-fishing these imitations when they are present is often just as effective. I like to carry a few nymph imitations—one dry that will hold up a dropper nymph and another for match-the-hatch situations.

The only stonefly present on the Bighorn is the Yellow Sally. Trout feed on the adults throughout the river.
JIM SCHOLLMEYER

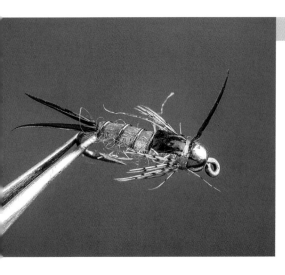

Kyle's Beadhead Yellow Sally

Hook:	#12-16 Daiichi 1710
Thread:	Tan 6/0 Uni
Abdomen:	Light cahill MFC Frog's Hair
Antennae:	Brown goose biot
Back:	Burnt orange MFC Swisher's Gator Hair
Bead:	Gold MFC brass bead
Legs:	Hungarian partridge
Rib:	Copper wire
Tail:	Brown goose biot
Thorax:	Yellow Wing N' Flash
Wing Case:	Black trash bag

Note: While this fly seems over the top at first look, this flashy nymph takes Bighorn trout readily, especially in fast-water riffles. It also fishes well under a large attractor pattern as a dropper nymph.

Garcia's Mini Hot Sally

Hook:	#16 Tiemco 200R
Thread:	Fl. chartreuse 70-denier UTC
Body:	Clear micro tubing
Hot Spot:	Red Flashabou
Underwing:	Pearl Ice Dub
Overwing:	Bleached elk hair
Hackle:	Brown saddle
Thorax:	Caddis green Ice Dub

Note: This fly sits flush on the water and the added sparkle gets the fish looking up. The fish don't see this pattern much, which I think adds to its effectiveness.

Idyl's Parachute Sally/Goldie Hawn

Hook:	#12-16 MFC 7000
Thread:	Light cahill 8/0 Uni
Body:	PMD MFC Frog's Hair
Butt:	Red 6/0 Uni
Hackle:	White hackle
Overwing:	Light dun saddle hackle
Post:	White MFC Widow's Web
Tail:	Light yellow mallard flank
Thorax:	PMD MFC Frog's Hair
Underwing:	Dun MFC Z-yarn

Note: This fly goes under different names depending on the manufacturer. It offers the most realistic silhouette of the natural on the water and is my favorite match-the-hatch dry-fly pattern.

Swisher's Parachute Madam X (PMX)

Hook:	#10-14 Tiemco 5212
Thread:	Tan 70-denier UTC
Tail:	Natural cow elk hair
Body:	Yellow Uni-Stretch Floss
Wing:	Natural cow elk body
Legs:	Brown round rubber legs (medium)
Post:	White poly yarn
Hackle:	Brown and grizzly rooster saddle or neck
Thorax:	Peacock herl

Note: This is a great attractor pattern all summer on the Bighorn and is especially effective during the Yellow Sally hatch. On the lower river, I frequently fish the yellow-bodied PMX with a nymph dropper.

Yellow Sally Fly Box

Nymphs
Kyle's Beadhead Yellow Sally (#12-14)
Tungsten Yellow Sally (#12-14)

Adults
Idyl's Parachute Sally (#12-16)
Garcia's Mini Hot Sally (#14-16)
Silverman's Parachute Sally (#12-14)
Swisher's Parachute Madam X (#10-14; yellow)

CADDIS

Caddis, like midges, also go through complete metamorphosis, and I carry several larva, pupa, and adult patterns. I also carry emergers to be fished in the surface film, egg-laying caddis with a pronounced egg sac and spent caddis that lie flat on the water. Breaking the code when surface fishing with caddis can be quite challenging. Trout create many different riseforms when eating caddis, so determining which pattern will work the best is often an exercise in trial and error.

Black Caddis

The Black Caddis (*Brachycentrus*) emergence is the most consistent summer hatch we have. They hatch daily toward the end of July through August, often lasting into September, and can emerge at any point throughout the day, depending on your location on the river. The Upper 3 is a great place to find Black Caddis emerging late in the morning. By the evening, right up until dusk, you will find this caddis emerging river-wide. The Black Caddis hatch tends to emerge all at once, often clouding up your view of the sky and turning your drift boat black. Fishing the Black Caddis hatch as the sun is falling below the horizon on a late summer evening is one of the most enjoyable fishing experiences you can find on the Bighorn.

Brachycentrus caddis form cases as larvae, referred to as cased caddis, that offer them protection while living along the river's bottom. Once the larvae crawl out of their cases, they rise to the water's surface as pupae, which have bright green abdomens. The Poodle Sniffer created by Bighorn River guide David Palmer represents this feature well.

Black Caddis do not break through the river's surface quite as abruptly as Tan Caddis. An emerger that rides in the film or a pupa dropped behind an adult work well to take advantage of this. Black Caddis adults also spend more time floating on the surface than other caddis species, which makes fishing adult patterns highly effective. Expert Bighorn River fly tier David Dill's CDC Caddis Adult is by far the most effective pattern for imitating these adults. His pattern is always the first fly that I tie on when fishing this hatch on the surface. If the fish are being exceptionally choosy, I fish Harrop's Caddis Emerger next. While these are my two most effective patterns, I carry a host of others for specific applications.

Black Caddis adults can become so thick that they mask other aquatic insects available to the trout at the same time. At times I have been fishing over fish that I thought were feeding on caddis adults, not realizing right away that the fish were actually eating spent mayfly spinners in the surface film. Always inspect the water's surface before making your fly selection when caddis are hatching.

After mating, female Black Caddis return to the water to deposit their eggs. These egg-laying, or diving, caddis, deposit their eggs on or below the surface. In the evenings when the legs of your waders are covered with Black Caddis eggs, fish a Fertile Caddis or other egg-laying caddis imitation with a prominent green segment on its rear.

When the hatch starts at the beginning of the season, the Black Caddis are usually fairly large (#16); as the season progresses, you will find them in progressively smaller sizes, all the way down to a #20. Tougher fishing on the surface typically coincides with the hatching insect's size getting smaller. Not simply because of the size but, more so, because of the fishing pressure.

During the summer the trout's daily feeding rhythm will coincide with the Black Caddis emergence. Anglers should be prepared to nymph with pupae.
JIM SCHOLLMEYER

Olive Flashback Pheasant Tail

Hook: #14-18 Dai-Riki 075
Thread: Olive 8/0 Uni
Body/Tail: Olive pheasant tail
Rib: Copper UTC Wire (small)
Thorax: Peacock herl

Note: Bighorn trout love this pattern when Black Caddis pupae are ascending to the surface, which seems counterintuitive since it's technically a mayfly imitation. For whatever reason, the trout seem to favor it more than any other Black Caddis pupa imitation. Fish the bead version in a dry-dropper rig and the non-bead version under an indicator.

Palmer's Poodle Sniffer

Hook: #16-18 Dai-Riki 135
Tail/Body: Black pheasant tail
Thread: Black 8/0 Uni
Rib: Chartreuse UTC Wire
            (Brassie)
Thorax: Peacock

Note: Created by former Bighorn Angler head guide David Palmer, the Poodle Sniffer is highly effective and easy to tie. The chartreuse wire is the key to its success, and it is almost as good as the Olive Flashback Pheasant Tail at imitating Black Caddis pupae.

Peacock Soft-Hackle

Hook: #16-20 Dai-Riki 070
Thread: Black 8/0 Uni
Rib: Krystal Flash
Body: Peacock herl
Hackle: Hungarian partridge

Note: The Peacock Soft-Hackle can be used to imitate a variety of insects on the Bighorn but works especially well during Black Caddis time. It can be fished under an indicator, swung in the surface film, or trailed behind a dry fly.

CDC Caddis

Hook: #16-20 Dai-Riki 305
Thread: Black 8/0 Uni
Body: Gray olive Hareline Micro
           Fine Dry Fly Dubbing
Wing: Dark dun premium CDC

Note: This is my go-to fly for fishing the Black Caddis hatch on top. I often tell anglers that if you are not catching fish on this fly, then your presentation is probably off—it works that well.

CDC Bubbleback Caddis

Hook:	#16-18 Tiemco 206 BL
Thread:	Black 8/0 Uni
Tail:	Sparse tuft of dubbing over wood duck fibers
Abdomen:	Black Trouthunter Caddis-Emerger-Nymph dubbing
Wing:	Black Trouthunter CDC
Legs:	Hungarian partridge
Thorax:	Black Trouthunter Caddis-Emerger-Nymph dubbing

Note: Another excellent pattern by René Harrop, this fly sits in the surface film and is great for fooling picky trout. I like to use this fly during thick hatches when trout may be keying in on the emerging insects.

CDC Caddis Emerger

Hook:	#16-20 Tiemco 100 SP BL
Thread:	Black 8/0 Uni
Shuck:	Black CDC fibers
Abdomen:	Black turkey biot
Legs:	Partridge fibers
Wing:	Black Trouthunter CDC
Antennae:	Two wood duck flank fibers
Head:	Black Trouthunter Caddis-Emerger-Nymph dubbing

Note: This René Harrop creation is another pattern that sits in the surface film and is effective over picky fish. I really like to use this pattern toward the end of the Black Caddis seasonal emergence when the fish have seen just about every other pattern.

Hemingway Caddis

Hook:	#16-20 Daiichi 1100
Thread:	Black 8/0 Uni
Rib:	Copper wire (extra fine)
Abdomen:	Gray beaver dubbing
Hackle:	Dark dun rooster neck
Underwing:	Wood duck flank
Overwing:	Canada goose secondary quill

Note: The Hemingway Caddis is a classic that continues to be effective year in and year out. It is probably the most popular Black Caddis adult sold on the Bighorn. Earlier on, you can fish the larger sizes. Later in the hatch the insects' size decreases, so fish a size 18 or 20.

Black Caddis Fly Box

Nymphs
Poodle Sniffer (#16-18)
Green Wire Pheasant Tail (#16-18)
Olive Flashback Pheasant Tail (#16-18)
Dill's Caddis Pupa (#16-18)

Emergers
CDC Bubbleback Caddis (#16-18; black)
CDC Caddis Emerger (#16-18)
YFG Caddis Emerger (#16-18; black)

Adults/Egg-Laying Caddis
Palmered Caddis (#16-18; black)
CDC Caddis (#16-20; black)
Fertile Caddis (#16-20)
Hemingway Caddis (#16-20; black, gray)

Tan Caddis

Tan Caddis, also called Spotted Sedge, do not hatch every year on the Bighorn, but when they do it may be the most enjoyable hatch of the year to fish. Similar to Yellow Sallies, *Hydropsyche* caddis require clean gravel and well-oxygenated water, which is why these hatches are also the best following high-water years. Tan Caddis arrive in July and last into October, with August and September the best months. Their large size—typically 14 and 16—along with their fluttering nature after emerging make them highly recognizable.

Spotted Sedge larvae do not have cases, making them easier offerings to the trout, but it is the pupae that are the most coveted underwater stage of the hatch. Once these yellow-bodied pupae ascend to the surface, they break through the surface film quickly. As a result, fish aggressively chase them and eat them right at the surface. You will often see large splashy rises throughout the river that look like dry-fly rises, but they are from trout keying in on the pupae breaking through the surface film. The Translucent Emerger by Scott Smith and the Emergent Sparkle Pupa by Gary LaFontaine are by far the two most effective emerging Tan Caddis patterns. I rarely fish this hatch without an emerger.

Once the caddis emerge as adults, they quickly make their way off the surface of the water. While the river's trout frequently eat high-riding adult imitations, it is highly effective to trail one of the caddis pupa emergers 16 to 18 inches behind your dry fly.

Unlike when fishing mayfly dry flies, where a drag-free drift is almost always necessary to fool a trout, it is often better to incorporate deliberate motion with your Tan Caddis imitations on the surface. Skittering your adult and slowly moving your pupa with short twitches are excellent techniques for inducing a strike. These short, abrupt movements make your imitations look like they are breaking their way through the surface film.

The last stage of the *Hydropsyche* life cycle is the egg-laying stage. Once this caddis lays their eggs, they remain with their wings spent on the surface. At this point the caddis is helpless and the trout find an easy meal. Mike Lawson created the Spent Partridge Caddis for this instance.

Besides the Yellow Sally hatch, the Tan Caddis emergence is the other hatch that is fished effectively with dry flies from a moving boat. The imitations are easily visible and the fish eat them in all areas of the river. You should always carry caddis imitations to mimic every stage of the life cycle for the most success. At some point during each day, the fish will be keying in on one of the specific stages mentioned above.

Trout key in on every phase of this emergence. Splashy rises will indicate trout feeding on the adults. JIM SCHOLLMEYER

LaFontaine Sparkle Pupa

Hook:	#14-16 Daiichi 1100
Thread:	Tan 6/0 Uni
Underbody/ Shuck:	Golden yellow Antron
Body:	Yellow-brown Antron
Wing:	Natural deer hair
Thorax:	Brown Australian possum dubbing

Note: This classic, created by the late Gary LaFontaine, perfectly represents an emerging caddis. You can fish it with or without a bead, depending on what part of the water column you are targeting. I like to fish this pattern with a tan, brown, or ginger body.

Translucent Emerger

Hook:	#14-16 Daiichi 1100
Thread:	Rusty brown 6/0 Danville
Rib:	Silver tinsel
Body:	Nature's Spirit caddis emerger dubbing
Beard:	Soft fibers on the bottom of the hackle stem
Wing:	Caribou

Note: This is the most deadly Tan Caddis pattern I have ever found. I can't explain exactly why it is so effective, but it has to do with the dubbing used for the body. You need to manicure this fly frequently to keep it fishing properly, but when presented well, this pattern does not get refused!

Double Duck Caddis

Hook: #14-18 Dai-Riki 305
Thread: Tan 8/0 Uni
Body: Rabbit dubbing (thick)
Overbody: Dark dun CDC
Wing: Tan CDC

Note: This fly rides low in the water and perfectly imitates an emerging adult caddis. The CDC used for this fly is the key to the pattern. This fly also fishes well for the Black Caddis hatch when tied with black dubbing.

Lawson's Spent Partridge Caddis

Hook: #14-16 Daiichi 1100
Thread: Tan 8/0 Uni
Abdomen: Tan Superfine Dubbing
Wing: Hungarian partridge body
            feathers
Hackle: Brown and grizzly rooster
            hackle
Thorax: Peacock herl

Note: When Bighorn fish key in on spent caddis, this is the one to fish. It has proven its effectiveness on rivers all over the West. If you are finding that fish are unresponsive to your offerings but your presentation is good, this fly will often break the code.

Tan Caddis Fly Box

Larvae/Pupae
LaFontaine Sparkle Pupa (#12-16; tan, ginger)
Hungarian Caddis Pupa (#12-16)
Translucent Pupa (#12-16)
Hare's Ear (#12-16)

Emergers/Adults
Translucent Emerger (#14-16; tan, brown)
X-Caddis (#12-16; tan)
Double Duck Caddis (#12-16)
Lawson's Spent Partridge Caddis (#12-16; tan)

TERRESTRIALS
Ants and Beetles
Ants and beetles offer excellent fishing opportunities throughout the summer. The flying ant hatch is definitely the most overlooked hatch on the river, and anglers rarely identify these terrestrial insects while fishing the Bighorn. The cottonwoods that line the Bighorn are a favorite habitat for flying ants. It is rare to actually see clouds of these insects in the air. I maybe encounter this only a few times a year. You are more likely to see individual ants flying around. The bottom line is that the fish know that they are present and have a fondness for eating them.

I regularly prospect with ants while fishing from the boat throughout the summer. Ants are my go-to dropper for fishing in side channels and flat surfaces from the boat. I fish imitations as large as size 12 in the shallow edges of the river, dropping a small beadhead nymph 24 inches behind. I tend to get the most fishing enjoyment out of fishing a small size 16 or 18 ant pattern over rising fish. My imitation often gets eaten opportunistically and is a great way to "unmatch" the hatch.

Beetles are present throughout the length of the Bighorn also. While beetles are not as prevalent as ants, trout on the Bighorn certainly feed on them throughout the summer. Some of the river's largest brown trout seem to have a great fondness for them. Beetle patterns are effective trailed behind grasshopper imitations.

Though often overlooked by anglers, ants and beetles are highly coveted insects by Bighorn trout during the summer.

Bloom's Flying Ant

Hook:	#12-16 Dai-Riki 305
Thread:	Dark brown 8/0 Uni
Body:	Black Frog's Hair Dubbing
Wing:	Gray Antron yarn
Post:	Fluorescent pink poly yarn
Hackle:	Grizzly

Note: All of Missouri River guide Dave Bloom's patterns are highly effective, and this is my favorite ant imitation for the Bighorn. It works well either blind-fished along the bank or over rising trout. This is a deadly pattern for the lower river in both black and cinnamon.

Hi-Vis Foam Beetle

Hook:	#10-16 Daiichi 1100
Thread:	Black 8/0 Uni
Back:	Black Fly Foam (2 mm)
Post:	Orange Fly Foam (2 mm)
Body:	Black Peacock Ice Dub
Legs:	Black rubber legs (optional)

Note: This pattern works well from May through September. I mostly fish beetle patterns trailed behind a grasshopper or on their own over rising trout.

GRASSHOPPERS

Starting as early as late June and lasting through September, hopper fishing is certainly one of the highlights of the fishing season. The hotter and windier the weather, the better the hopper fishing will typically be. Each summer, hot and dry conditions force grasshoppers down to the water's edge to feed on lush riparian vegetation, where they are susceptible to being blown into the water. This is often aided by afternoon breezes, welcomed by both anglers and the trout. Smooth, glassy flows and shallow riffles lend themselves perfectly to watching rainbow and brown trout attack these large dry flies off the surface.

Grasshoppers are often of great importance to both anglers and trout alike on the lower river. With the diminished density of aquatic insects in the lower river, terrestrials represent a large percentage of the diet of trout that inhabit the lower river in midsummer. The lower river from Bighorn Access to Two Leggins is surrounded by prime agricultural land in which these terrestrials thrive. When fishing the lower river during the summer, I am rarely without a terrestrial on the end of my line. I also find that trout in the lower river respond well to a "twitched" terrestrial imitation where the angler incorporates movement into the imitation. A hopper dropper rig with a beadhead nymph dropped 20 to 24 inches below the grasshopper imitation is especially effective in the riffles.

The most popular sizes for hoppers on the Bighorn are anywhere from size 8 to 14, with 10 and 12 used most frequently. It seems that once the fish become accustomed to seeing more and more hopper imitations, the smaller sizes become more effective. Body color is another important variable. While a grasshopper underside changes color throughout its life, we have found that tan, yellow, and peach imitations are the most effective on the Bighorn.

Grasshoppers provide exciting surface fishing on the Bighorn from July through September. While epic hatches of grasshoppers don't occur every year, they usually produce some of the most fun fishing. JAY NICHOLS

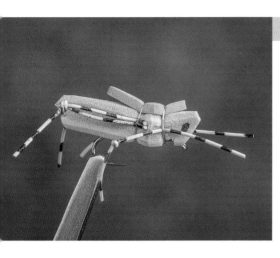

Morrish Hopper

Hook:	#8-12 Dai-Riki 730
Thread:	Tan 140-denier UTC
Body:	Gold (2 mm) and tan (4 mm) foam
Legs:	White/black Hareline Zebra Legs
Post:	Orange foam (2 mm)

Note: This pattern has become a go-to hopper pattern throughout Montana. It comes in a wide variety of colors that all work well at one point or another during the summer, including gold, tan, pink, and black.

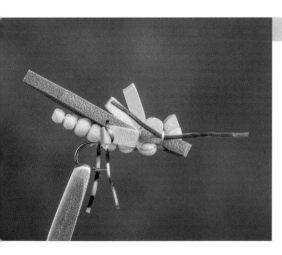

Shanafelt's Mongo Hopper

Hook:	#10-12 Dai-Riki 280
Thread:	Tan 6/0 Uni
Body:	Peach Fly Foam (2 mm)
Wing:	Dark brown Fly Foam (2 mm)
Back Legs:	Tan speckled Sexi-Floss, tan foam (1 mm)
Front Legs:	Tan Flexi Floss
Indicator:	Yellow and orange foam

Note: Created by Bighorn Angler co-owner Pete Shanafelt, this hopper floats well and has great body segmentation. It is effective with a peach or tan body.

Schroeder's Parachute Hopper

Hook:	#10-14 Tiemco 5212
Thread:	Tan 6/0 Uni
Post:	White calf body
Hackle:	Grizzly rooster saddle
Rib:	Brown Uni-Stretch Floss
Abdomen:	Tan Antron Dubbing
Wing:	Turkey wing or tail
Legs:	Knotted ringneck pheasant tail fibers
Thorax:	Tan Antron Dubbing

Note: This classic, natural-looking hopper pattern works well every year with a tan body.

Panty Dropper Hopper

Hook:	#10-14 Daiichi 1100
Thread:	Tan 6/0 Uni
Body:	Orange and brown foam (2 mm)
Wing:	White packaging foam
Back Legs:	Red barred Flexi Floss knotted to tan foam (1 mm)
Post:	Orange Fly Foam (2 mm)
Front Legs:	Tan barred Flexi Floss

Note: This fly rides low in the water and has a silhouette unlike any other hopper on the market. The tan body and red legs make it irresistible to the trout. It has quickly become a go-to hopper pattern.

White Cloud Hopper

Hook:	#8-12 Daiichi 1100
Thread:	Tan 6/0 Uni
Body:	Peach and tan foam (2 mm) marked with Sharpie
Legs:	Natural round rubber legs
Underwing:	Yellow Swiss Straw
Wing:	Tan Spectrum Wing
Overwing:	White Widow's Web

Note: I really like the profile of this hopper on the water, and it's easy to see. The peach spotted body seems to be the key to its effectiveness.

CHAPTER 6

Nymph Fishing

A properly set-up nymph rig, in the hands of a master nymph fisherman, is simply deadly on the Bighorn River. Though it might not be as glamorous to some as dry-fly fishing, nymph fishing can keep you into fish all day and is often responsible for producing the largest trout of the year on the Bighorn, especially rainbow trout.

The Bighorn River is a nymph fly fisher's dream. An endless supply of trout-filled river features await, perfectly suited to being fished with a nymph. Seams, drop-offs, riffles, inside bends, runs, and pools all hold an abundance of trout. Dead-drift nymph fishing with a strike indicator, split shot, and two flies is the most popular form of nymphing on the Bighorn. Other opportunities exist to Czech nymph, sight-nymph, and swing soft-hackles.

The Bighorn's size may intimidate some the first time they approach it. Anglers who routinely fish small limestone creeks in Pennsylvania, streams in the Sierras, or Driftless Area spring creeks do really well here—they don't look at the river as a massive Western river, but instead break it down by its features and determine where the trout will hold within that water. Once you have done that, you can calculate your approach and adjust your tactics based on the type of water you have chosen. Once you have had success in a particular area, it will be easier to recognize other similar stretches that should hold fish also.

If there is a lack of hatching insects, you are unable to spot trout feeding on nymphs, or the surface of the water doesn't contain any nymphal shucks, then you should approach the water with the idea that the trout are feeding opportunistically. Remember, opportunistic feeding tends to coincide with searching or blind-fishing the water with your nymphs. It is best to select generalist imitations that represent various food sources. After catching a few fish and making various fly changes, you should be able to hone your fly selection until you are consistently taking trout.

Nymph fishing is by far the most used tactic for catching trout on the Bighorn, and for good reason—it results in trout to the net 365 days a year. The best nymph anglers on the river cover as much water as possible, make weight adjustments, and religiously clean moss off their flies. JAY NICHOLS

If emerging insects are present, you can visually identify feeding fish, the surface film contains recently discarded nymphal shucks, or your stomach pump reveals a trout's fondness for one particular organism, select a nymph that accurately represents what you are seeing. At this point it is safe to say that the trout are most likely feeding selectively. If this is the case, then I choose to fish my imitative nymph below a more general pattern to cover all my bases.

There is a lot of food under the surface of the water, and fish will feed in lies where they can use the least amount of effort to consume the largest quantity of food. This is often in amazingly shallow water close to the bank or in the slowest part of the river close to where you may initially think of standing. Before stepping foot in the water, look for these fish; even if you don't see them, make a few drifts close to you. Many anglers new to the river stand where they should be presenting their fly, and you will routinely hear guides tell their clients that they are "walking on the fish"—there was most likely a fish where they were standing before they rushed too far out into the river.

The speed of sound in water is six times faster than the speed of sound in air. Because of the Bighorn's calm nature, trout can detect the most subtle movements by anglers whether in a boat or on foot from a long way away. Always take the time to cautiously approach the water you are about to fish. When fishing a riffle, you may push the fish out as you get into position, but because of the abundance of food and the amount of angling pressure, these fish will often move back into their feeding lanes fairly quickly if you don't create any further disturbance. Be patient and observe the fish and the water thoroughly.

Once you determine the trout's position and how it is feeding, adjust your rig accordingly. The first thing I do is adjust my indicator placement on the leader according to the water depth. On even riffles and smooth, wide runs, it is not as crucial to move your indicator as it is when you are fishing seams and drop-offs. There have been countless times when a client has stepped out of the boat to fish a spot with no success, but as soon as I adjust the indicator, the same drifts catch fish.

The same rules apply to the amount of weight affixed to the leader—"the difference between a good nymph fisherman and a great nymph fisherman is one split shot." Because of the abundance of food in the river, the trout do not have to move much at all to consume calories. Getting your flies down in front of the fish is crucial, and small, continual adjustments can lead to great success. Because the river bottom is relatively smooth, consisting of cobble and small gravel, you are far less likely to snag (and lose) your rig, so going too heavy at first with your weight is typically not an issue.

Bighorn trout feed efficiently in shallow water where it is easy for them to consume calories. Anglers will find excellent nymph fishing, especially sight-nymphing, in shallow riffles and runs. Here Bighorn Trout Shop head guide Merritt Harris fishes such a run. HALE HARRIS

In general, your approach will be more calculated when fishing a slot, seam, or current edge versus an expansive riffle or run. In certain lies, the fish will be more congregated and the feeding lane much more defined. Pay extra attention to your setup in these situations. You have fewer margins for error in the way you are rigged in such areas.

Riffles, seams, gravel bars, mid-river shelves, current edges, and long runs are all good nymph fishing water. It is especially important to take notice of the color change in the water; the first thing that I look for when I step into a run is the change to darker water that signals depth. A color change from darker water to lighter water is also present when areas of the bottom covered in vegetation give way to areas of only rock. Look for this characteristic in the summer when the growth of aquatic vegetation is at its peak. This transition zone is also a dead giveaway that trout are present. In these areas you will often find the fish on the gravel or right up against the vegetation. When you approach a run on foot or from the boat, always look for this color change. The river's clear water provides you this advantage.

Equipment

The right equipment will allow you to cover the water most efficiently. Five- and six-weight fast-action rods are ideal. Four-weight rods are growing increasingly popular, as rods increase in length and become faster in action. A six-weight rod is my preferred weight for nymphing the Bighorn because it allows me to turn over longer leaders, split shot, and strike indicators with ease.

While nymphing with a 9-foot rod will work well, 9-foot, 6-inch and 10-foot rods are great for this large tailwater and are ideal for casting just about any nymph rig, controlling your drift, and most importantly, mending your line. I find that 9-foot, 6-inch rods are the best all-around tool for every nymph fishing situation on the river. The extra 6 inches allows me to manipulate my line that much better than a 9-foot rod, yet doesn't create the fatigue of casting a 10-foot rod all day.

I find that 10-foot nymph rods are best for high-stick nymphing where shorter casts or even roll casts are used most often. On the Bighorn, this is typical when fishing current edges and drop-offs, when you want as much line off the water as possible to reduce drag. These rods are also well suited for sight-nymphing and using short-line nymphing techniques in the riffles. Because of the length, I like to go with a rod rated for a 4- or 5-weight line, which gives you excellent feel and control when nymph fishing.

Your fly line is often one of the most important aspects of nymph fishing. Having the right line match up to the rod and the situation you are fishing is imperative for turning over your nymph rig and managing your drift once on the water. Weight-forward fly lines with heavier, short front tapers, or longer belly lines with an indicator tip, have become the most popular lines today for nymph fishing.

Sight-Nymphing

The Bighorn River provides anglers with the ability to sight-fish unlike any other river I know, yet not many anglers do it. Though you can sight-fish to trout feeding on the surface, most often you will be hunting and presenting flies to trout feeding subsurface, and stealth is paramount.

Training your eyes to spot fish takes time and practice. This practice can be easily acquired by watching the water intently each and every time you approach. Look for subtle movements, out-of-place spots or colors along the river bottom, or a flash of the trout's underside and/or the white of the trout's mouth, which can be seen when the trout takes an insect. A high-quality pair of polarized sunglasses is vital to identifying these trout giveaways. When you are fishing, these same movements will be your clue to set the hook, not a strike indicator.

Approach the water cautiously and stalk the fish from the bank. Fish where others are not—in overlooked, out-of-the-way shallows, inside bends, and along the edges of seams. Take the time to cover water on foot, hunting for trout in areas undisturbed by other anglers. These out-of-the-way places often hold the largest trout.

Stealth and observation are the keys to locating fish to cast to. The last thing you want to do is walk into the water aimlessly, moving fish from their feeding lie. When the sun is high, you can easily spot fish in the water; unfortunately, that is the easiest time for trout to spot you as well. Approaching fish when you are casting a long shadow across the water can be difficult. By approaching the fish in their blind spot, typically from behind their location, you can use the sun to your advantage without them being aware of your presence.

A fish feeding on nymphs may actually be closer to you and deeper than it appears through the water. Cast far enough upstream with a dry-dropper rig or a skinny water nymph rig (no indicator) to let your nymph get down to the fish. Landing your fly on its head may easily spook it away. Try to be slightly behind the fish in one of the trout's blind spots when presenting your fly. Casting down to the fish from an upstream position will often put you or your rod within their cone-shaped field of vision. ■

Longer rods, large arbor reels, and fly lines with long front tapers are all beneficial for nymphing. PAUL RUHTER

These more heavily weighted fly lines, with shorter front tapers, will load fast-action rods well because they are weighted one-half line size heavier than marked and will turn over your indicator nymph rigs with ease. Great examples are the Rio Grand or Airflo Xceed fly lines. If you are only to have one line for dry-fly and nymph fishing, I recommend one of these. There are also several nymph-specific fly lines on the market today such as the Rio Indicator II and Airflo Nymph/Indicator Line that have longer bellies and longer, thicker tapers ideal for mending and controlling line on the water.

Long Line Rig

The long line indicator nymph rig is the most commonly used and covers most nymph fishing situations. You can wade or fish from the boat with the same setup, which includes a 9-foot leader, strike indicator, split shot, and two flies. The overall length of the setup is typically between 11 or 12 feet from the top of your leader to your bottom fly. The typical distance between the strike indicator and the split shot is between 8 and 9 feet.

My nymph setup starts with a 9-foot 3X or 4X nylon leader. I find no need to fish a fluorocarbon leader on the Bighorn and do not know of a single guide who uses one. I like to choose a leader that is one size heavier than my tippet size to make turnover as easy as possible. From the end of my leader, I tie on a 16- to 18-inch section of fluorocarbon tippet to my first fly. I like to use a fluorocarbon material for my tippet due to its knot strength, abrasion resistance, and invisibility underwater. From that first fly, I then tie on another section of 16- to 18-inch tippet to my second or bottom fly.

I tie the tippet that is attached to the second fly to the eye of the first hook. I prefer tying to the eye rather than the bend because I feel the fly will act more naturally in the water and it is easier to free weeds from the top fly. If you hold the tippet on each side of the top fly tight, then "thwack" the line with your thumbs, the weeds will come right off the fly.

In general, I typically use 4X to my top fly, which is usually some form of a scud or sow bug pattern, and 5X to my bottom fly, which is typically a small nymph, pupa, or midge imitation. When fishing worms and large scuds as a top fly, I increase my tippet to 3X. My tippet to my bottom fly rarely changes unless I am fishing two sow bugs or larger impressionistic nymph patterns, such as caddis pupae or Yellow Sally nymphs, in which case I increase my tippet to 4X. I rarely go lighter than 5X when nymphing, unless I am sight-nymphing with tiny midge or mayfly imitations.

When tying my fluorocarbon tippet to my nylon leader, I will use an improved blood knot or triple surgeon's knot. I use the blood knot when tying on tippet material to a leader of similar diameter. When dealing with a situation where the diameters of material vary greatly, I use the triple surgeon's knot. Another way to attach your tippet material to your leader is with a tippet ring or small barrel swivel at the junction point of your leader

The long line indicator nymph rig is often used by Bighorn guides when nymph fishing from a drift boat. HALE HARRIS

Regardless of the water you are fishing and the nymph setup you choose to incorporate, a drag-free drift is a must when nymph fishing the Bighorn. HALE HARRIS

and tippet with clinch knots. This method is becoming increasingly popular because you can make use of your leader for a longer period of time, since break-offs will occur where your tippet attaches to the swivel.

Your tippet to leader knot not only joins your two lines together, but also acts as a stop for your weight. The most popular weights used on the Bighorn are lead split shot and tungsten putty. I personally use split shot, because I like to apply a precisely measured amount of weight. It is easy to quickly remove a piece or add another. Anglers who prefer putty find that it attracts fewer weeds and places less of a hinge point in the leader. I carry a range of split shot that includes sizes 0, 2, 4, and 6—0 being the largest and 6 being the smallest. These sizes are found in the yellow and orange Super Doux split shot assortments. Size B and BB Water Gremlin split shot are also useful.

Your indicator choice is really a personal preference, be it yarn, cork, foam, plastic, or latex. I, like many others, use Thingamabobbers. They float well and are relatively easy to cast, easy to see on the water, and sensitive enough to detect subtle takes. I fish the ³/₄-inch Thingamabobber most of the time; when I am fishing slow water in the spring or sight-nymphing, I will drop down to the smaller $1/2$-inch size. Latex balloons are also popular. While harder to prepare and attach to your line than a Thingamabobber, they offer better floatation and are more sensitive to strikes, which is why many guides prefer them.

Shallow Water and Dry Dropper

Shallow water nymph fishing was brought to tailwater rivers by successful spring creek anglers and is most effective in shallow water riffles before an insect emergence, while sight-nymphing, or when fishing to trout that have moved into shallow, well-oxygenated riffles during the summer. These shallow water areas provide sight-nymphing opportunities and hold some of the largest trout in the river, but often go untouched at peak times.

This rig is short, often no more than 6 feet long from the indicator to the bottom fly. I start with a small Palsa Pinch on Float or small yarn indicator. The smallest Thingamabobber is OK to use in choppy water. From my strike indicator, I drop 2 to 4 feet of 4X tippet to my first fly and then another 14 to 16 inches to the bottom fly. The weight is often minimal—for this setup I use size 4 and 6 split shot or a dab of tungsten putty.

When fishing a dry-dropper rig, the dry fly acts as a natural strike indicator, suspending the nymph at just the right level where the trout is holding. I find the dry-dropper technique to be one of the most enjoyable ways to fish the Bighorn. When I introduce the dry-dropper method to clients who don't have past experience with this technique, they seem to find it highly rewarding also.

I use the dry-dropper technique most often in the summer, when fish have moved into oxygenated riffles or are in the shallows tight to the bank to feed. The dry-dropper technique is often a better summer technique than the shallow water nymph rig because you also have the opportunity to get a surface take. It is also a better boat-fishing alternative to the shallow water nymphing technique, mainly because you can present your setup tighter to the bank. The only time I feel that this is the opposite is in the spring, primarily during the Blue-Winged Olive emergence, when trout are feeding more selectively. Trout will move into the shallows, along banks, and in riffles to feed on nymphs and emerging nymphs. The dry-dropper technique is predominantly used while wading, when sight-fishing, and in skinny shallow water where stealth is of the utmost importance.

A buoyant attractor pattern, such as a grasshopper or other terrestrial imitation, is usually used as the dry fly because it floats well and looks natural on the water. A size 12 Parachute Ant is my preferred dry fly—the trout take them on the surface well. But ants don't float as well as other foam attractors or terrestrials and can easily be pulled underneath by a bad presentation, so they require more maintenance.

Here an angler demonstrates perfect line management while achieving a great drift with his nymphs. While nymph fishing is the easiest way to get beginning anglers into fish on the Bighorn, good nymph fishers are highly skilled technical anglers who have mastered the nuances of subsurface fishing. You can match the hatch just the same as you can on the surface and use tactics that will continue to challenge—and reward you—in every season.
HALE HARRIS

I typically suspend my nymph 20 to 24 inches below the dry fly, even when fishing water that is a foot or less deep. I find that when fishing a beadhead nymph it still takes time for the nymph to sink, and the trout will react right away in water of less than a foot. When it is deeper—say two to three feet in depth—you are still deep enough. Trout in the shallows often hit the nymph right after it hits the surface water, and the take is often confused as a dry-fly take.

I use three patterns almost exclusively for the dropper. The first is the Tungsten Split Case PMD, which works well at imitating emerging mayfly nymphs in general, as does my second, a Mercer's Micro Mayfly. Something about this fly takes fish better than all others—even a standard Pheasant Tail—when used as a dropper. Maybe it is the compact profile or the epoxy back fished just below the surface film. The last is a small, black Tungteaser, which sinks well and represents midge or Black Caddis pupae.

Achieving Your Drift

Regardless of what nymph fishing tactic you use, a flawless, drag-free drift will result in fish to the net. Mending mitigates line drag and is the most important technique to master to become a good nymph fisherman. Drag occurs when your line and flies are moving faster or slower than the current. This drag on your line in turn drags your flies, making them look unnatural to the trout. A mend corrects this by repositioning your fly line on the water in the opposite direction your line is being pulled by the current. If your fly is floating in faster water than you are in, you need to mend up to slow down your drift. If your fly is in slower water than you are in, you need to mend down to accelerate your drift.

Besides mending, line management is the most crucial element to nymphing success. Line management is the practice of using slack line to achieve a better presentation of your fly. Managing your line properly takes a lot of time get right. When nymph fishing, you want to carry a good amount of extra line off your reel to feed into your drift. As your indicator is drifting, if you don't have enough slack in your drift, your line will drag. If you have too much slack in your drift, you won't be able to set your hook properly.

Watching your strike indicator intently through the whole drift is important. Good nymph fishers are always maintaining good "contact"

A good, firm hook set the moment you detect a strike is the key to landing fish on the Bighorn. HALE HARRIS

with their flies throughout their drift by keeping a close eye on their indicator and line. Active nymph fishers are always managing their line, either bringing line in or feeding line out, depending on where they are in the drift sequence, to get the best drift possible.

Proper mending and line management are best demonstrated on the water, but I will describe a typical sequence. Cast your indicator rig upstream and out into the current. After your flies hit the water, you should have slack in your line hand and some on the water to feed into your drift. As the indicator starts to come toward you, hold your rod tip high to keep the slack off the water. When the drift is about to come even with you, mend your slack line upstream, getting all of your fly line upstream of your indicator. This step is crucial in setting up the rest of your drift; if your fly line is below the indicator, the current will create drag on your line rather quickly, ending the effectiveness of your drift.

Once your indicator starts going below you, begin laying slack line on the water with a series of small upstream mends to feed your drift down-river. This is referred to as stack mending. Once your drift is even with you, or just past you, you are most likely to get a strike. At this point, your flies should be on the bottom and drifting drag-free. Keep your eye on the bobber. Continue feeding line through a series of small upstream mends and rod tip shakes until your indicator drags out. In many instances, with the ability to stack mend well, you can effectively cover 20 to 30 feet below you. This is the most efficient way to cover the most amount of water with each drift. Always adapt your mending technique and your amount of slack line, depending on the speed of the water and the currents you are fishing.

When using a long line indicator nymph rig, your flies are not right under your strike indicator during the drift—they are actually out and at a slight upstream angle from where your strike indicator is located. When you cast your rig upstream, your split shot sinks quickly to the bottom, where the speed of the current is slower. This is occurring simultaneously to your strike indicator moving more quickly in the surface current. When this occurs, the split shot and your flies are upstream and at an angle from your strike indicator. During the drift, your split shot should be ticking along the bottom and your flies should be slightly up off the bottom. If at any point throughout your drift your indicator moves in the slightest or hesitates, set the hook immediately. In slower water, or when water temperatures are in the upper 30s or low 40s, these movements are often slight. When setting the hook, I like to bring my rod straight up and simultaneously pull my line tight with my offhand. If you strike too low to the side, you may get resistance from your indicator against the surface of the water, prohibiting a good hook set.

CHAPTER 7

Dry-Fly Fishing

The dry-fly season on the Bighorn starts as early as February, with abundant midge emergences, and extends through November. Due to variances in seasonal emergences, the timing of each hatch is not always the same from one year to the next. Often the best times are the last two weeks of April and the first two weeks of May for spring dry-fly fishing, the last two weeks of July and the first two weeks of August for summer dry-fly fishing, and the last two weeks of September and the first two weeks of October for fall dry-fly fishing. With that being said, these "windows" often attract the most angling pressure. The shoulder times between these windows, based on the timing of the hatches, also provide great dry-fly opportunities.

Anglers that have the most dry-fly success are the ones who go out on the river each day well prepared to fish dry flies and are looking specifically for rising fish. During the peak times of insect emergences, the dry opportunities will be blatantly evident and river-wide. During shoulder occurrences, the time of day and location of the rising trout may be limited, but still very present. During these shoulder periods, having up-to-date information or a guide who is in tune with the river's dry-fly rhythm is key. Unlike many Montana rivers, active surface feeding can occur without any perceptible hatch being present in the air or on the water. The light conditions may make seeing insects difficult. The hatch or spinner fall may have occurred upstream and not be happening where you are standing. These conditions can make matching the hatch particularly difficult, and often a lot of changing flies is necessary before the particular insect and stage the trout are feeding on are discovered. A phone call to one of the area fly shops will get you started off on the right foot and help you develop a strategy before you hit the water. Regardless of the time of year, an understanding of trout behavior and how the fish respond to the insect hatches can be crucial, and collecting as much information as you can before hitting the river will bring you that much closer to success.

157

The Bighorn River offers anglers one of the longest dry-fly seasons in the West. Capturing a trout with a dry fly on the Bighorn is one of the most rewarding fly-fishing experiences an angler can experience. The spring creek characteristics of a tailwater such as the Bighorn present their own set of circumstances and challenges to the dry-fly angler. HALE HARRIS

Once on the water, the Bighorn's relatively slow water velocity, abundance of insects, relatively high angling pressure, and clear water will all present challenges. Each time you stand within casting distance of a rising fish, or a pod of rising fish (as is often the case on the Bighorn), you will have to figure out and overcome numerous variables at any given time. Breaking this code with a dry fly often requires that several elements come together harmoniously.

Success begins before ever making a cast, and observation is the most important element. Before I even think about rigging my rod for the day, I take into consideration the air and water temperature and how they influence an emergence, based on the time of the year. These two factors will often determine what hatches will occur, what time of day an emergence will start, and how long its duration will be.

Once I hit the water, the next thing I look for are signs of insects, either dead or alive. The surface film will provide you with more clues than anywhere else in regard to dry-fly fishing. Your seine is an invaluable tool for collecting bugs on and just below the surface. Examining the air and streamside vegetation can also offer clues as to available insects and the stage of the emergence. Armed with such clues, you can then start your search for rising trout.

Before casting my line, I always look for a target. Blind-fishing or flock shooting a small dry fly during a match-the-hatch period can be the kiss of death. It can either put down potential rising trout or lead to a total waste of time fishing an area where there are no trout, or where the trout have no intent of rising to a dry fly. The only time I choose to blind-fish is during summer emergences or when terrestrials are present.

Whether walking the bank or floating in a drift boat, I begin searching for rising fish along the river's edge, in current seams, flats, tailouts, edges of riffles, foam lines, and anywhere else dead bugs collect or insects drift in the current. On the Bighorn River, you will typically find fish feeding in pods, usually in a group of six to eighteen fish, with the number of fish in a pod increasing with the intensity of the hatch. Fishing a pod presents its own challenges. It is important to single out an individual fish, typically the biggest, by trying to identify its size from a tail or head, depending on how it is taking the insect. Don't rely on the size of the ring or surface disturbance. The largest trout have been conditioned to feed in an efficient way that is undetectable to predators. If they all seem to be the same size, you should work on the fish closest to you. Once you have isolated a single fish, you can begin to determine what insect and what stage of a particular insect emergence the fish is keying in on. Working on the fish closest to you will hopefully keep you from spooking the other fish as a result of your casting or with the madness that ensues after a take.

Individually feeding fish are typically found tight to the bank, whether by a cliff wall or Russian olive bush or in skinny water on the edge of a

A calculated approach and accurate presentation go a long way to achieving success as a dry-fly fisherman. Here an angler works a pod of trout in the Landing Strip. HALE HARRIS

Here the author displays a brown trout that ate a hopper tight to the bank from a moving drift boat between Bighorn Access and Mallard's Landing Access. TROY HUMPHREY

riffle. The difficulty of fishing to a single fish is that if you put that one down, you often have to move and locate a fish in a totally different area—unlike pods, where if you put one down, there will be more targets still within reach. When casting to a single fish, your first cast needs to be your best cast.

Once you locate the fish, you need to be able to determine which of the insects present the trout are feeding on and which stage of the emergence the trout are taking. These two aspects of the hunt will be critical to your dry-fly success, and if you can't do this, you can be left frustrated, confused, and often fishless. You may be fishing the right insect, just not imitating the proper stage of the emergence, or you may be fishing an imitation of the wrong insect in a hatch of several, such as when Blue-Winged Olives are hatching and the trout are taking midge clusters, when or Tricos are emerging and fish are eating PMD spinners.

You won't always "break the code" on a particular fish or on any given day. Sometimes the fish beat us, and that's OK. Use these experiences as learning tools for the next day or the next fish you encounter. Often trial and error by switching fly patterns will result in catching fish, and that is why it is important to have patterns for each stage of the hatch. If it isn't your fly pattern, look at how you are rigged, how you are presenting your fly, or from where you are presenting your fly. All of these aspects are crucial to success. Don't do the same thing that isn't working over and over again and expect that things will change.

The next aspect of breaking the code is learning to identify the trout's riseform, which is an important clue in determining what stage of the hatch a fish is feeding on and making the right fly selection. For example, if a trout is feeding on Blue-Winged Olive nymphs just below the surface— which, by the way, is a characteristic of larger trout—and only disclosing its tail when feeding in the surface feeding zone, that trout is typically going to refuse even a well-presented, high-riding dun imitation. The anglers not having success dry-fly fishing an emergence are often not identifying this activity.

Fish feeding in the film or just below the surface can be taking any combination of emerging nymphs, emerging duns, cripples, or spinners trapped in or just below the surface film, a 3-inch transition zone where it is highly efficient for the trout to feed. When trout are feeding on these highly susceptible insects, they give away clues as to what stage of the emergence they are feeding on by the way they consume the natural insect. When trout are feeding exclusively below the surface, say on midge pupae unable to penetrate the surface film, you will typically only see the trout's tail break the surface. When trout are feeding on insects in the film, for example floating mayfly nymphs or emerging duns, only the tail or dorsal fin will break the surface. Many of the largest trout on the river feed in this manner because it is so efficient. When trout are feeding on spinners or duns on the surface, you will often see only the mouth or nose of the trout break the surface of the water.

Dead or crippled insects floating on the surface or in the surface film are easy pickings for Bighorn trout. Here an angler displays a nice rainbow that was feeding on spent spinners in the slack water along the river's edge.

The Presentation

While a preliminary reconnaissance and a calculated approach are vital to success, when push comes to shove, the presentation is everything. The first thing you want to consider is the position from which you are going to present your fly to the rising trout. Because many times the river will dictate your approach based on which side you are on, the speed of the current, and the type of lie the trout is feeding in, it is important to be able to present your fly from any casting position and/or angle.

Mastering the down and across or straight upstream presentations should be your top priorities. I prefer to fish dry flies down and across when possible. You will most often find yourself presenting your fly from this position when you are dry-fly fishing from the boat, whether anchored or moving, or working rising fish while wading a flat, where you have the room to do so. When fishing down and across, the main error that I see anglers make is casting too far and lining the fish. On flat water and small insects, that is usually game over. Accurately judging the distance to your target comes with practice, but there are a few things you can do to make

Fishing your dry fly down and across with a reach cast is the key to effectively presenting a dry fly from a drift boat. If you don't present your fly downstream ahead of the boat, drag will quickly occur. PAUL RUHTER

sure this doesn't happen. I always present a drift or two short of the rising fish to help gauge my distance before I attempt to put my fly over the fish. When fishing across to a target, laying your fly on the water short of the target will rarely, if ever, put the fish down. This allows you to settle down and get the jitters out before actually casting to the fish.

The straight upstream approach is highly effective while wade fishing pods, on the edge of a riffle, in a seam, or along the bank. The upstream approach is also the stealthiest. If you stalk your fish cautiously, you can get close to your target. Regardless of which approach you choose, you should try to position yourself as close to the fish as possible. Take heed of the best angler on the river, the great blue heron. A slow, calculated approach will serve you much better than a mad dash into the water. Move slowly and be patient when approaching the fish, and at no point start flock shooting while you are moving toward your target. Once you are in the best possible position, start your presentation. If at all possible, try not to enter the water at all before presenting your fly. Any unnecessary movements can easily be detected by the trout.

Regardless of the position from which you are presenting your fly, achieving a drag-free drift through slack line casts and aerial mends is critical, except when imitating caddis and terrestrials. I use the reach cast and tuck cast in almost every dry-fly cast. Slack line casts allow you to manipulate your fly line in the air so that the fly floats drag-free from the moment it hits the water. Mending your fly once it hits the water, especially when you are playing the small fly game, is a major no-no. Becoming proficient with these advanced casts is the most important element of presentation that will turn a good caster into a great dry-fly fisherman.

Just like golfers go to the driving range to practice using their clubs, anglers should go out in their yard or in local water and master the reach cast and all other casts. Becoming proficient at performing the reach cast is the number one thing you can do to become a better fly fisher. It is vital to being a good dry-fly angler. Extending your arm to the left or right as you stop on your forward cast performs the reach cast. The stop of your rod will dictate where your fly lands, and the follow-through to the left or the right will determine where your line lands in relation to the fly. This allows you to position your fly line before it ever lands on the water. This air mend also enables you to place your fly line well above the fly, while still placing your fly right on target. What this means is that you are fishing your fly well the second it hits the water and often no further line management is necessary during the entire drift.

When performing a down and across presentation, having your fly line land above your fly on the water produces a significantly longer drag-free drift than if you had cast straight across. If you cast your fly straight across without a reach cast, your fly line is going to have the tendency to drag immediately and will often put down your targeted fish. If you try to mend your way out of a straight-across cast, you will most likely sink your fly. On straight-up presentations, the reach cast often keeps you from lining the fish. When you make your reach right or left, your line will fall to the side of the trout's line and your fly will still land right on target. I find that the reach cast is an indispensable tool for the fly angler.

The tuck cast allows you to drop your fly to the water with an abundance of slack in your fly line and leader when it lands on the water. This slack line cast enables you to overcome the tendency of the surface currents to drag your fly line, resulting in a long, flawless, drag-free drift to the fish. Mastering these advanced casts will allow you to present your fly effectively when it counts most—on the first cast—and cover water as efficiently as possible.

The timing and placement of your fly over the fish is also important. Once you locate rising trout, examine the rhythm and frequency of their feeding behavior. When fish are in pods, they are typically more likely to feed in a steady rhythm than single fish, which can be more selective, looking for a particular stage of an emergence or feeding when there are fewer insects to eat. Once you have determined the trout's rhythm, decide on the placement of the fly, which can vary anywhere from one to four feet in front of the fish, depending upon the location and frequency of the feeding. When a trout is in choppy water, or feeding in a frequent rhythm, the distance I lead the fish is shorter than when a trout is feeding selectively in flat water. Regardless of how far upriver you lead the fish, you must place your fly in the trout's exact feeding lane. When trout are feeding rhythmically to insects on the surface, they rarely move far side to side to take a fly. The closer to the surface of the water a trout is, the smaller its field of vision becomes. This is why casting accuracy is once again so important.

My final thought on presenting a dry fly may be the simplest and most important tip of all. If you can't see your fly on the surface of the water, do not make another cast. Bring your fly in and dry it off. Anglers tend to get in the same frenzy that the trout are in and start casting in rapid succession. Often their fly has been sunk for the past six drifts. Even if the trout took the fly, they would have no idea. Small dry flies are hard enough to see as it is. Dry and manicure your flies regularly, even if it's every other drift. This will also slow you down and allow you to assess the situation in front of you more accurately, and will probably result in a better presentation.

Picking the right color of fly, or post, can also be key. In differing light conditions and glare, the standard white post becomes difficult or impossible to see. Sometimes you can position yourself to get a different angle of light, but this is not always the case. Posts with bright, highly visible colors such as orange, yellow, chartreuse, and pink often have good visibility in the bright glare of a sunny day when the water looks like a bright silver mirror. Black or gray posts help overcome dark or black glare

While fly pattern selection is critical when dry-fly fishing, presentation of your fly is all that matters in the end. JAY NICHOLS

when there is overcast light, shadow, or the sun is low in the sky, causing the light to hit the water at a sharp angle.

To manage extreme glare, it is often best to work as a team, with one angler fishing and the other acting as spotter, finding an angle on the bank where the flies can be seen and directing casts and when to strike from that vantage point. Fishing with a guide who has well-trained eyes is invaluable when dry-fly fishing in poor light conditions.

Equipment and Rigging

When deciding on a dry-fly rod, I look for two things: feel and accuracy. I prefer medium-fast and fast-action rods, with stout butt sections and slightly softer tips. These faster action rods allow you to turn over long, delicate leaders and easily manipulate your fly line in the air.

I prefer a 4-weight rod in the 8- to 9-foot range for match-the-hatch dry-fly fishing on the Bighorn. I find shorter rods to be more accurate and precise when presenting your dry fly. Longer 9-foot rods are useful when making long drifts over varying currents. Most often you are presenting a dry fly between 25 to 35 feet and 40 to 45 feet at the longest. I find the shorter rods are better at this range. When fishing on windy days or with larger dry flies such as grasshoppers, I prefer 5- or 6-weight rods. Rods suited for heavier line weights are also great when fishing dry flies from a moving boat, when presentations need to be presented quickly and accurately.

A good dry-fly reel has the lowest possible start-up inertia. Having as little hesitation as possible from your reel after you hook a Bighorn trout will help protect the fine tippets often needed when dry-fly fishing. A large arbor reel is also helpful to maximize your ability to retrieve line as quickly as possible after a large trout has made a run. The 3-Tand TF and Hatch Finatic Series are my reels of choice.

I like lines that are easily manipulated with aerial mends during reach and tuck casts. I also want a line that loads the rod quickly, yet lands softly on the water. Every major manufacturer makes lines with dry-fly-specific tapers that aid the caster in doing these things well. The Rio Trout LT and Airflo Elite lines are two of my favorites.

The overall length of my dry-fly leaders are in the 9- to 12-foot range. I select a leader one size heavier than the tippet I will be fishing to achieve the best possible turnover. If I am fishing a 5X tippet, I like to use a 4X leader. Extra-long 16-foot dry-fly leaders aren't necessary, but your leader needs to be formulated properly to help you achieve a drag-free drift, and a longer section of fine tippet will help greatly in reducing micro drag on the surface, giving you a better presentation. This is important when dry-fly

My favorite dry-fly rod for the Bighorn is an 8-foot, 6-inch, 4-weight with a crisp action that allows me to present my fly accurately. Here Bighorn Angler guide Seth Byler works a pod of rising fish in the Gravel Pit. JAY NICHOLS

fishing on the flats, where the slightest surface disturbance will spook the fish. When fishing size 18 to 22 flies, you should be prepared to fish down to 6X tippet. I strictly use Trouthunter tippet for many reasons, such as strength and abrasion resistance, but one of the main reasons is the ability to fish tippet in half sizes. It sounds a little over the top I know, but I can often get away with fishing 5.5X instead of 6X in quite a few situations, giving me—and more importantly, my clients—added hook set and fish fighting strength. Though rare, I sometimes have to drop down below 6X in the most technical situations, and I have much more confidence in 6.5X than 7X.

I use a combination of products to keep my flies visible on the surface. The first is Fly Agra, a pretreatment liquid that is a combination of mucilin and lighter fluid, which I use on all types of flies except for those with CDC wings. After you dunk your fly and make your first false cast, the lighter fluid evaporates and what's left behind is a coating of mucilin, which works brilliantly as a waterproofing agent for your fly. Fly-Agra and other waterproofing agents are often most effective when applied twenty-four hours before fishing. I usually dip the flies in Fly-Agra and leave them out overnight to dry. I prefer to use Loon Lochsa or Shimazaki Dry Magic for initially treating CDC flies.

Once my fly is soaked from presenting the fly or from landing a trout, I immediately use an amadou patch. This fungus, which is harvested from trees in France, is an excellent natural drying agent and something I could not dry-fly fish without. Once my fly is dry again, I use a desiccant such as Frog's Fanny or Fly Duster to manicure my fly before casting again. Manicuring your fly with a desiccant is especially important when fishing CDC patterns. If the CDC is mashed together, the material will lose its ability to effectively float the fly. Drying and fluffing out CDC with desiccant using a brush is the most effective way of rehabilitating them.

Pattern Selection

There are three keys to pattern selection, regardless of what water you are on: size, shape, and color. If you adhere to these three characteristics, you will be in the ball game. Regardless of the hatch I am fishing, I tend to lean toward more subtle or sparse patterns on the Bighorn. I find that they are simply more effective at fooling the most discerning trout. Many of these sparse patterns sit low in the water, looking much more natural to the fish, yet remaining highly visible to the angler.

Many of my most successful dry flies for the Bighorn River incorporate CDC in some way. This material is highly buoyant, has a sleek profile, and is extremely durable. René Harrop revolutionized the use of CDC in fly patterns. His highly effective fly patterns were created to fool the most elusive Henry's Fork trout, and their effectiveness crosses over beautifully to the Bighorn.

CHAPTER 8

Streamer Fishing

It is hard to have confidence in streamer fishing until you have been successful with it. While anglers often streamer fish to go after some of the largest trout, at the right times it can bring quantity as well as quality to the net. The Bighorn River is one of the most consistent streamer fisheries there is.

The best times to fish streamers are early in the year—February and March—and then again in the fall, right before and after the brown trout spawn. On the Bighorn, this spawn occurs later than most, so fall streamer fishing will be best in October and November. In the summer, an overlooked time to fish streamers on the Bighorn, diehard streamer fishermen can find great success on smaller, more neutral imitations, especially during years of high recruitment of juvenile fish. Larger trout will forage on these smaller trout year-round. Matching your streamer technique and fly patterns to variables such as river type, water clarity, weather, and water temperature will have a significant impact on your success rate.

Casting proficiency is probably the most important element of streamer fishing. Whether fishing the banks or a mid-river structure, from the boat or on foot, your ability to place your fly in likely holding areas is going to be one of the critical keys to success. More often than not, the more spots you hit, the more fish you will have move to your fly.

There are many ways to present your streamer—from pounding the banks to slow and deep strips, long strips, short strips, strip-strip-pause, mend and twitch, dead-drift, and swing. All of these techniques have their place when fishing the Bighorn, based on the water you are fishing, the temperature of the water, and the time of year.

A little common sense goes a long way when deciding which method will work best the day you are on the river. If water temperatures are optimal for trout activity—46 to 60 degrees—you can expect fish to be more active than if the water is 38 degrees (on the cold side) or 68 (on the warm side). When temperatures are within their optimal range, the trout

Guide Josh Edwards displays a nice lower-river rainbow that ate a Sparkle Minnow fished on a sink tip in the early spring.

often welcome a faster, more aggressive presentation. The one time that I will slow down my retrieve, even if water temperatures are within the optimal range, is when the water temperature is falling. Trout will react to this and often become less aggressive on the Bighorn.

In the winter and early spring I tend to fish slower and deeper, when water temperatures are on the colder side of the optimal range, or when a significant temperature change has occurred. At this time, I typically incorporate longer and slower strips, often in the deepest part of the run, because the trout's metabolism will have slowed down considerably. When fishing deep, I like to use full sinking fly lines (250 or 300 grain) to ensure that my fly gets down quickly to the bottom and stays there. These heavier lines can be laborious to cast but worth the effort. When fishing deep, I also often fish two streamers of different characteristics, since I am covering a less defined area of water. Being methodical in your approach is key when fishing this way. Cover as much water as you can, and be as diligent as possible. When water temperatures are in their optimal range, in late spring or in the fall, your retrieves can be more erratic and quicker. Trout will be spread throughout the river, holding in a variety of water types. This is when you can get the great surface strikes and big boils along the banks.

Streamer fishing turns on through the lower river when water is rising or clarity diminishes during runoff. At this time fish will often move tight to the banks, where clarity can sometimes be better. Prime streamer fishing on the banks often occurs when the river is dropping and just

This rainbow ate a Home Invader fished slow and methodically through a deep run near the Grey Cliffs.

clearing. As visibility improves, it is time to pound the banks hard. This is a great time to move a big one down low.

Fishing the banks is a game of inches, and precision casts will bring you the most success. I like to key in on structures, seams, undercuts, and drop-offs within 2 feet of the bank. I typically do the best pounding the banks when water temperatures are ideal for trout—in the 50s or so. Your strips are typically fast and erratic and your arm should be thoroughly worn out at the end of the day from presenting your fly to the bank as many times as possible. The gravel-based water right near the shore should be your target area. Making a cast inches from the shore and stripping across this gravel area into the green-bottomed area can elicit vicious strikes. Also, cast into the still pockets of water right next to the shore. Large trout hold in these quiet bodies of water, waiting for an unsuspecting small fish to become their next meal. These pockets can be found along cliffs, where creeks enter, behind snags, or anywhere you find a current break or protection.

When fishing the banks, floating or intermediate fly lines tend to work the best. This is when we typically get the most explosive takes and what I call kill shots—there isn't any chase to the boat; you just hit your spot with the fly, the fish immediately reacts, the line goes tight, and the fish is on. If you are getting several chases from the fish but no kill shots, first change the pace and action of your strip. If that does not work, change your fly.

Another technique I like to use is a dead-drift and/or mend and twitch approach. This approach is fished slower and works well in drop-offs, seams, around mid-river rocks, and when fishing runs out of a boat. For example, when you come upon a mid-river boulder you will have deeper holding water in front of, on the sides, and behind the boulder as well as in the accompanying downstream seam. Fish will sit in all of these. The dead-drift and twitch approach allows you to quickly get your streamer down to the fish around the likely structure.

Your ability to manipulate your line through mending will allow you to get your fly deep in the hole and, most importantly, keep it there. Once it's in the strike zone, you can impart action to your fly, in association with the plunging action of the current, through short twitches. Keeping your fly down and sliding off the rocks increases your catch rate and is an effective technique when imitating the abundant populations of leeches that hold tight to the river bottom.

Bighorn brown trout are aggressive and readily take streamers fished in a variety of ways. This fish ate a Lil Kim pattern fished in a relatively shallow riffle. JAY NICHOLS

Equipment and Rigging

For streamers, I typically use a 9-foot, 6-, 7-, or 8-weight fast-action fly rod.
I tend to lean more toward the heavier rods, because then my casting tool
never limits me. On a 7- or 8-weight rod, you can effectively cast and turn
over any line or fly you will need. The weight of the rod I use is dictated
by the size of fly I am going to use and the water that I am fishing. Deep,
fast water requires heavier flies, which in turn require a heavier line and a
rod rated for that line.

For most of my streamer fishing, I fish a forward segment of sinking
fly line in front of a floating line. I have two sinking lines (or a sink tip)
ready to fish at all times, one with a 15-foot sink tip and another with a
24-foot sink tip. I like my streamer lines to have a sink rate of 3 to 8 inches
per second (ips). The 15-foot line is the best all-around streamer line,
typically of an intermediate sink rate, and the most user friendly. It is easy
to pick up off the water, shoots line well, and is effective at getting your fly
down in a wide variety of water. The longer line with a 24-foot sinking
section is most frequently used in the winter or early spring season when I
need to keep my fly down on the bottom or when I'm fishing heavy
currents. I also use this longer tip when I fish the lower river, where deep
holes are more common. In some of the largest, deepest holes in the
Bighorn, a full sinking line is necessary to be most effective.

When water temperatures are warmer throughout the summer or early
fall and fish are more apt to move a long distance to chase a fly, I often
fish weight-forward floating lines with short front tapers and weighted one

Guide Seth Byler rigs a 300-grain sinking line on a large arbor reel to be fished on a stout 8-weight rod. JAY NICHOLS

line size heavier. These lines are ideal for loading the rod quickly and turning over large or heavy streamers.

For anglers who don't want to invest in an additional reel, spool, or sinking line, sink tips that you can attach to your floating fly line work fairly well. I always use a sink tip of 7 or 10 feet in length. Longer tips become difficult to cast with a floating fly line. These sink tips come in sink rates ranging from 3 to 7 ips and can cover a wide variety of streamer fishing conditions and match well with many different rod actions and weights. I most often use the Rio 5.6 ips, 7-foot sinking leader.

Off the end of my sink tip, or full sinking lines, I fish heavy 4- to 6-foot monofilament and fluorocarbon leaders. For the butt section of my leader, I use heavy 30- or 35-pound Maxima monofilament. From here I quickly taper my leader down to fluorocarbon tippet. There is no need to go light here—12- to 20-pound-test tippets are ideal. I prefer fluorocarbon tippets because of their superior abrasion resistance. Just be sure you don't make your leader too long for the water you are fishing. If you use too long of a leader in deep water, your sinking line will go down and your fly will take longer to sink because the length of your leader is making your fly lag behind. My leaders are often as short as 4 feet and never longer than 6 feet when fishing small, subtle patterns.

Pattern Selection

If there is one rule for streamer pattern selection, it is to fish the fly you have confidence in. We all have a fondness for a certain fly that has brought success in the past. Your ability to present your fly, not the pattern itself, will decide your success fishing streamers on the Bighorn most of the time. Often it is best to go with your instinct. If a pattern worked well once, why not again? I always enjoy changing flies and trying new patterns, but I definitely have certain trends I seem to follow when it comes to selecting the right streamer pattern.

Common traits I look for in a streamer pattern are movement of the fly in the water, silhouette, and color. I have a thing for flies tied with rabbit strips and marabou. These materials move or "breathe" extremely well in the water. I also like deer-hair heads, which push water and attract fish, especially in dirty water. One of my favorite patterns also incorporates lead in its body, which allows the fly to wobble in the water, making the fly act as if it's injured.

Carry a wide selection of flies in various silhouettes and colors. There is nothing wrong with trial and error. If you have fished through good-looking water and haven't turned a fish, don't hesitate to change to a different pattern or color. Keep your hooks sharp and fish hard.

Using the Drift Boat as a Tool

Fishing from a drift boat is a team effort. Both anglers need to communicate well and effectively do their job for the most success. A drift boat is only as good as the person rowing it. This is why many people hire a guide when fishing the Bighorn. An oarsman's ability to row the boat at the speed at which the current is moving the angler's drift is imperative, otherwise the flies will drag and the angler will spend more time casting than fishing their drift.

The oarsman is also responsible for making sure that the boat is in the proper position (both orientation/angle of the boat and distance from target) to fish a particular spot. The worst thing you can do is float through a prime piece of water too quickly. It is imperative that the rower slows the boat down so the angler has ample opportunity to achieve a good drift. Hiring a well-qualified fishing guide will allow you to get the most out of fishing from a drift boat on the Bighorn.

With the boat in the right position and moving at the proper speed, it is the angler's job to make a quality presentation. When fishing from the drift boat, not only do you have access to more water, you can also get a better drift through that water. Casting is often easier from a drift boat, as long as anglers are mindful of their boat mates. With two anglers casting in close proximity, it is important to cast at the same parallel angle to avoid tangling. When fishing nymphs from the boat, I like to have my clients cast at a 90-degree angle straight out from the side of the boat. After the flies hit the water, the angler should immediately mend to put slack in the line between the strike indicator and the end of the rod. This slack allows the oarsman to row the drift for a significant distance before it is necessary to re-cast. The angler can make slight adjustments of the line when needed. The faster the water, the more line management is needed because the current will be more likely to drag your fly line.

When fishing dry flies from the boat, I like my anglers to cast at a slight downstream angle with a reach cast, which ensures that your fly line lands upstream of your fly and lengthens your drift. If you cast straight across, your fly will immediately drag. When fishing from a moving boat, anticipate your next cast so you are prepared to make the proper presentation in the right spot. Again, a good guide will coach you on when and where to make your presentation. ■

CHAPTER 9

Wisdom of the Guides

John Sindland

John gained a passion for dry-fly fishing on his home waters in Connecticut. He made his way West to be closer to such great dry-fly rivers as the Bighorn and Henry's Fork. He has called Fort Smith home for over a decade, where he guides for Bighorn Angler.

What advice would you give dry-fly anglers?

The most important thing is to set up on the fish properly, paying attention to sun, wind, current, and other things that would allow yourself to get the best drift because it's really all about the drift. Don't cast too long initially or line the fish. Work a pod of fish correctly by starting with the back ones first and not just casting immediately over all the fish. Take the time to realize what cast might be the best.

What are the most significant changes you have seen in the Bighorn over the years?

How hatches have come and gone and come back. When I moved here in 1990, I was amazed by how Tricos, PMDs, and Sallies were great some years, same with the caddis. When the river hit low flows and had silting issues, the hatches went away. When we started getting better flows, it was amazing how the hatches returned. There was a point in the late 1990s and early 2000s you wouldn't have PMDs. The flies just disappeared, we didn't have the hatches, and the Bighorn became primarily a nymphing river. Now that we've had good flows and good flushes, the habitat has come back.

The Bighorn River is a dry-fly angler's dream come true. Intense insect emergences and trout willing to rise for a fly are the key ingredients. Here midges cluster around a drift boat.
HALE HARRIS

Why the Bighorn, Fort Smith?

It's one of the best trout fisheries in the lower 48, and if you were going to design a fishery with the habitat, the water flows, the wadeability, and being able to use a boat, you couldn't, in my mind, draw up a better river.

What are the benefits of guiding on the Bighorn, and what makes it such a great fishery?

Getting to know it so intimately and how it always evolves. It might not seem like it changes a lot, but the guides who really play the game right— get out and hunt fish on a regular basis—know how the little micro spots change. You find little nooks and crannies where sometimes the fish really surprise you in what they provide out of a small corner. When you are guiding all the time and talking to other guides, you realize how much it changes from March to fall and late winter and from year to year. Anglers that have become intimate with the river see these changes and enjoy that.

Why should a person hire a guide, and what makes a good fishing guide?

The guides know the water and know it better than you do. A good guide is able to read his client, and knows when to push them a little bit, when to pull back. All clients are not created equal and they want different things; a good guide has patience, understanding, and doesn't rip into them when they screw up.

What makes for a good client, and what can anglers do to make the most of their guide trip?

A good client is willing to learn, listens to what you recommend, and tries to take it to the next level. No matter their skill level, there's usually something you can show them and maybe they can show you sometimes. Once you hire a guide, don't make decisions for him. Some days start out great and some days start out slower, so sometimes you have to be patient.

What are some of your favorite patterns?

Roger Heil's Crippled Thor and Frank Johnson's Student. They can be tied to cover any mayfly. The CDC Caddis. For nymphing, a Ray Charles and a Quill Nymph.

What mistakes do you commonly see people make?

Wading out too far is one of the cardinal sins for me. Many anglers don't pay attention to their surroundings and don't notice what is 6 inches or a foot off the bank. People think they need to fish the middle of the river, not realizing they just walked through many fish to get to a few fish.

What comes to mind when I mention drag and line control?

Being able to recognize drag, or more specifically micro drag, is maybe one of the most difficult things, even as you advance as an angler. It's so subtle; but it is the difference between a great drift and a good drift, and that difference is sometimes what it takes to catch fish.

How can a good fly caster become a better fisherman?

If a fish is in a difficult spot and a person can do an aerial mend, being a better caster certainly helps, but I've had a lot of clients that weren't great casters but were great fishermen. They knew how to use their weakness and were able to present the fly properly with the tools they had. Instead of casting 30 feet, they waded carefully into position so they only had to cast 20 feet.

What, if anything, would you do to change the Bighorn?

Try to maintain the minimum flow levels we need during drought conditions. The flows make a tremendous difference with our hatches and spawning habitat. Second is etiquette. We all, even guides, could maybe be a little more patient. Don't be afraid to share patterns, or share the river and don't sit in a run all day.

Adam Berg

Having grown up in eastern Montana, Adam was exposed to all of its outdoor splendor from a very young age. His passion for hunting and fishing became his career in 1998 when he started guiding for Eagle's Nest Lodge.

What's the most important thing you teach beginners when they get in your boat?

I teach them to get in and out, and how to stand safely in the knee braces while fishing. Safety first. Then I coach them on how to achieve the proper drift from the boat. To get a good drift from the boat, you don't have to cast far. Being able to properly mend is the most important element of achieving a good drift. I work on that first.

What advice would you give dry-fly anglers fishing the Bighorn?

Practice casting accurately at 30 to 40 feet. Just like hitting the driving range before a round of golf, practicing your casting before going on a major fishing trip will go a long way toward being successful. Whether it's hitting just the right seam when fishing nymphs from the boat or accurately presenting a dry fly, an angler needs to be able to consistently put their fly in a 6-inch window.

Hiring a guide for a day of fishing on the Bighorn should be on everyone's bucket list. A good guide is in tune with the daily rhythm of the river and can ensure you have great **success.** HALE HARRIS

What is the most important piece of equipment the angler should have?
Fishing on the Bighorn is a visual experience. A good pair of polarized sunglasses will help you read water, spot fish, and keep your eyes safe from hooks. I have seen people get hooked in the eye . . . not fun. Also, a stiff rod. It always helps when fishing from the boat or dealing with the wind.

What are the benefits of guiding on the Bighorn, and what makes it such a great fishery?
I have called this area home for a long time, and I couldn't imagine guiding anywhere else. The fishing is consistent year in and year out, and because of that we have the longest guide season in the state. Endless guide trips on the best fishery in the world! The habitat for trout is unmatched anywhere. Consistently cold water throughout the year, tons of food, and being able to share the river with many likeminded catch-and-release fishermen.

What is your favorite season and/or hatch?
July has always been one of my favorite months. The river and the fishing are in full swing. Spring runoff is over and the water temperatures climb into the 50s. These warmer water temperatures create abundant insect hatches that make the fish active and feed aggressively.

Why should anglers hire a guide, and what makes a good fishing guide?
Being successful on the Bighorn is all in the details. There are a lot of little things an angler can do that will make the difference between catching a couple fish and clobbering them. I'm a self-taught fly fisherman; it is hard, and takes lots of practice to get good at. After fly fishing and guiding for several decades, I can now teach a client in three days what took me many years to learn. A good guide is a good teacher. The true test of a good guide is if your people want to fish with you again. When a person leaves a better angler than when they came, they usually come back and fish with you again.

What makes for a good client, and what can anglers do to make the most of their guide trip?
Leave your ego at home and bring a positive attitude. We all know everyone has tough days on the river. I would rather take a poor angler with a good attitude over a good angler with a poor attitude. If you want to have a good day with your guide, trust him and listen to him. Even if he is just an average guide, he still knows more about the Bighorn than you do.

What are some of your favorite fly patterns for fishing the Bighorn?
A big white streamer. Some days this fly is not the best choice for numbers
of fish, but it is by far the most exciting! In the clear flows of the Bighorn,
it is easy to follow a white streamer as you strip it through the water.
When a fish follows and takes your fly, you see the whole thing. It is an
awesome experience.

What mistakes do you commonly see anglers make?
Too short of a drift, and fishing with moss on your flies. You simply will
not catch any fish on the Bighorn if you have moss on your flies. Check
and clean your flies regularly. Don't be lazy—keep your flies clean, fish
more, and cast less. Knowing how to manage slack line, being able to feed
line into your drift, and being able to stack mend will result in you
catching more fish.

How can a good fly caster become a better trout fisherman?
Anglers become better through time on the water and observing everything
around them, including how the trout are behaving, what hatches are
coming off, and understanding where and how trout feed. Being with a
good guide and learning how to master the different angling techniques
will shorten that learning curve.

What should people do to prepare for the Bighorn?
Practice the timing of your cast. Ninety percent of fly fishermen rush the
cast and come forward too quickly on the forward cast. If you are fishing
with an indicator nymph rig, you will be punished with lots of tangles.

What, if anything, would you do to change the Bighorn?
I would get rid of rental boats. Not to say those folks don't have a right to
be there, but on a river as busy as the Bighorn, people that do not know
how to ethically navigate a river cause a lot of inadvertent problems. I
have witnessed inexperienced oarsmen run into other wade anglers and
guide boats, and I have even seen a few sunken boats in my time. Not
good for anyone, and frankly not safe at times, either.

Hale Harris

Hale Harris grew up in Wyoming just a short distance from the Bighorn River. He has been the co-owner of the Bighorn Trout Shop in Fort Smith for nearly thirty years. His experience and knowledge of the Bighorn are unparalled.

What is it about Bighorn Lake that creates a blue-ribbon trout fishery below Afterbay Dam?

A large, deep lake coupled with a bottom-release dam almost always creates thermal advantages for trout. Quite simply, water temperatures stay cooler in the summer and warmer in the winter, and this benefits both trout and aquatic insects. That being said, it is the limestone geology of the Bighorn River watershed that is largely responsible for the world-class fishery. It creates an alkaline water chemistry that encourages weed growth, and this provides an almost ideal habitat for a variety of crustaceans and aquatic insects.

What is your ideal flow for fishing the Bighorn and why?

Somewhere around 4,000 cfs or slightly above is great. This maintains adequate flows in the side channels, and side channels are important for the overall health of the river. Side channels provide additional habitat for trout and aquatic insects, plus they are especially important for the recruitment of juvenile trout. They also can provide outstanding fishing

The quality of the fishing on the Bighorn is often dependent upon water flows. Here an angler prepares to nymph fish a riffle on the upper river at an ideal flow around 4,000 cfs.
HALE HARRIS

opportunities, especially for dry-fly fishing. Flows in the 5,000 or 6,000 cfs range are even better as it pertains to long-term fish numbers, but the main river can become less wadable at these higher flows.

How does water temperature affect the fishing and timing of the hatches throughout the year?

Generally speaking, high-water years bring warmer water temperatures and low-water years bring colder. This surprises some anglers, as it is usually just the opposite on non-tailwater rivers. The issue is thermal stratification in the lake. The bottom strata of lake water is the coldest. During high-runoff years, the sheer volume of water moving through the lake tends to flush out this bottom layer of cold water earlier in the summer. When this happens, water temperatures rise, and the warmer water temperatures move the hatch schedule up. For example, PMDs may hatch in July during high-water years, but could be pushed back to late August in low-water years. Black Caddis will be the main event in August during high-water years, but are a September, early October hatch when the water is low. Also, *Baetis* mayflies are usually a dependable spring and fall hatch. While this is still the case during low- or high-water years, they tend to sputter off throughout the entire summer when the water is low. So anglers who are planning to target a certain hatch need to be aware of this low-water/high-water dynamic and how it affects hatch timing.

What is the appeal of fishing the lower river (below Bighorn Access), and why should anglers consider fishing this section?

The river below Bighorn Access can be outstanding, but you have to take the time to learn it, and you have to pick the right times to fish it. The most obvious appeal is the relative lack of angling pressure. Probably 90 percent of anglers target the upper 13 miles, and for good reason. The upper river is consistently excellent, with a huge fish population, superb hatches, and almost no water clarity issues. As you travel downriver, the quality of the habitat decreases due to silt-laden feeder streams, irrigation return, and rising water temperatures. This has an adverse effect on aquatic insects and fish spawning success. Despite these negatives, if you were to consider the Bighorn to Mallard's section as its own river, a strong case could be made for including it as one of the top five fisheries in the state of Montana. It often provides great fishing with substantially more solitude. You often have the luxury of "cherry picking" your runs on the lower river because of the lack of angling competition. All this applies to the next section down: Mallard's to Two Leggins. The fishing can be excellent here too, but water quality degrades further. There are additional feeder streams and irrigation return to contend with. I have caught trout 15 miles downstream of Hardin, but trout numbers are low down there.

What are the most important issues facing the sustainability of the Bighorn as a world-class trout fishery?

Because of the river's incredible fertility and storied history, it is tempting to think of the Bighorn as an anvil that will wear out many hammers. However, we must be alert and work hard to be good stewards of this fishery. Water flows are the main factor dictating fish populations. Quite simply, high water means high fish populations, and vice versa. Mother Nature holds the cards overall, but how flows are managed by the Bureau of Reclamation (BuRec) is an ongoing issue. Currently, BuRec seems to be managing the Bighorn watershed in such a way that a full lake is the priority. This management policy lends itself to more extreme flows, both high and low. If the lake is full or in the flood pool, high runoff or a significant weather event will force BuRec to react by releasing huge amounts of water. This can cause erosion of stream banks and scouring of the streambed itself. During dry years, flows can be reduced to a trickle in an attempt to store water. If efforts were made to moderate river flows, this would greatly benefit the fishery overall. Also, "flushing flows" could be coordinated with the BuRec, especially during low-water years. This would eliminate siltation buildup in the river. Siltation adversely affects spawning success, particularly downriver, and it causes problems with aquatic insect species.

There have been discussions on building settling ponds and rerouting irrigation water to address water quality issues on the lower river. If these problems could be solved, it would create additional blue-ribbon trout water, spread out angling traffic, and enhance the fishing experience of many anglers. Whether engineering and financial concerns prove insurmountable remains to be seen.

Issues such as organic pollution, changing regulations, and local politics all present challenges as we go forward, but the future is bright.

What is the importance of fishing emerger patterns over rising fish on the Bighorn?

Experienced anglers have observed that in almost every insect hatch there is a time when the insect is most vulnerable to trout. For example, during the *Baetis* mayfly hatch the nymph rises to the surface, where the dun proceeds to extricate itself from the nymphal shuck. Depending on weather conditions, this transition can take some time—the insect may even become trapped in the shuck for a moment. Instinctively, trout are conditioned to concentrate on this most vulnerable stage, as they can feed more efficiently and expend less energy. Since it is common for trout to ignore upright duns in favor of emergers, anglers have devised fly patterns that imitate these emergers, and often enjoy great success. What I just described applies to all the Bighorn River's mayfly hatches. During caddis emergences, trout often target the pupae rather than the winged adults, so it pays to learn your entomology, and to be able to recognize different riseforms and what they reveal.

In the thirty years that you have owned a fly shop and guide service on the Bighorn, how have you seen the culture of our sport change?
It is slowly changing. Shop owners and others in the outdoor industry need to be proactive in bringing young people into the sport. Kids that used to be raised as sportsmen are declining in number. There are other interests out there capturing the attention of our young people—computer games and social media come to mind. We also need to be aware of our aging population and how this will affect the future. Baby Boomers have provided the bulk of our business over the years, and they are a large, affluent group. But as they age and become unable to participate, who will replace them? We can all recognize that demographics and economics pose some challenges.

Younger fly anglers are diverse. On one hand we have those who are conditioned by computer games and multimedia to expect immediate results or instant stimulation. These people may struggle with the patience required to become an accomplished angler and truly value the sport of fly fishing. Yet, others have been raised with good conservation ethics and an appreciation for the environment, and it is these people who are the future of our sport. So overall, there are changes, but both good and bad.

Brent Downey

With his father as one of the river's longest standing outfitters, Brent's whole life has revolved around the pulse of the Bighorn River. You can find him working side by side with his dad at Angler's Edge Outfitters in Fort Smith.

What's the most important thing you teach beginners when they get in your boat?
To look at it as you are here to have fun, no pressure, just have fun . . . and don't fall out. I teach them how to cast and all that stuff too, but most importantly they are here to enjoy themselves.

What advice would you give dry-fly anglers fishing the Bighorn?
Be patient. Fish don't always rise when you want them to. Try to pay attention to sources like the Internet and fishing reports. See when the hatches are peaking and plan around the hatches if that's why they are really there. The good thing about the Bighorn is you can usually find fish rising somewhere, even when hatches aren't at their peak—but be patient.

What are the most significant changes you have seen in the Bighorn over the years?
Fishing pressure has increased enormously. More outside guiding from non-local areas, guides coming up from Colorado, Wyoming, and other parts of Montana. This pressure is expected with fishing as good as it is.

What is your most memorable fishing day, for yourself or with a client?
I had a client catch a 29-inch, 10-pound rainbow on a size 18 Trico spinner in 1993. It's the highlight of my guiding career so far. I was young then and thought this is how it would be all the time. It fought harder in the net than it did on the line. It got a bunch of moss on its head and stopped fighting, and he just reeled it up. Then it hit the net and really started shaking. It was pretty cool.

What is your favorite season and/or hatch to fish on the Bighorn?
Tricos and the fall season in general. Match-the-hatch fishing with small flies is at its best. Tricos in the morning and caddis sometimes in the afternoon. The Trico spinner falls are pretty awesome.

Why should anglers hire a guide, and what makes a good fishing guide?
You can't beat local knowledge, no matter where you are coming from and how much experience you have. If you only have a short time to fish the river, it's better to go with someone who knows the river intimately rather than trying to wing it.

Fall is a magical time to be on the Bighorn. With water temperatures remaining much higher in the fall than on other rivers, ideal conditions exist for abundant late-season insect emergences. JAY NICHOLS

A good fishing guide has patience. You have to be able to accommodate different personalities, and a guide has to have somewhat of a personality, too. You can't be a bump on a log or people won't want to go with you again.

What makes for a good client, and what can anglers do to make the most of their guide trip?
A good client listens and doesn't contest and challenge everything you say. An open mind makes for a good client, but that's a two-way street. I've learned a lot from clients, too. Don't be afraid to ask questions and take advantage of the knowledge the guide has.

What are some of your favorite fly patterns for the Bighorn?
An orange scud is one of my go-to flies. The Wonder Nymph, midge clusters, and spinners. If any fish is rising, you can usually toss a spinner over them and get them to eat it. Hoppers, too—I love hoppers.

What mistakes do you commonly see anglers make?
Standing on the fish, wading out too far, casting to the middle of the river when the fish are often behind them. I also see some people crowding others a little too much. But the biggest one is more people wade beyond where they should.

How can a good fly caster become a better trout fisherman?
Pay attention—there's more than one way to catch a fish. Try to think like a fish. That's what separates the 90 percent and the 10 percent . . . 10 percent of the anglers catch 90 percent of the fish, and that's what does it—having almost what's like a hunter's instinct where you stalk your prey. It can be a personal thing between you and a fish.

What should people do to prepare for the Bighorn?
Know your limitations and come with an open mind. Don't have such high expectations. The Bighorn has gotten a reputation for people being able to catch a hundred fish a day, but that's not going to happen every day and skill has a lot to do with it. One thing you can do is prepare for the weather. It can change on a dime. I've had a lot of trips ruined because people didn't bring a rain jacket.

What, if anything, would you do to change the Bighorn?
Keep flows higher to keep back channels open for more habitats for the small fish to grow. Etiquette is a hard thing to teach. You see some rude stuff out there. It would be nice to have a little less of that, as well as not allowing people to fish the spawning beds.

David Palmer

David grew up in eastern Montana, where he fell in love with fishing at a very young age. After trying a career in the real world, he settled in as a fishing guide with the Bighorn Angler in Fort Smith.

What are the advantages of hiring a guide when fishing the Bighorn?

Guides are on the river almost every day. They understand its subtleties. They understand which water is fishing best at the time and which water isn't. Many guides know how to keep people out of crowds when it's busy. A lot of the guides are also really good at working with people. If a person is a novice, a guide can bring their skill and confidence up in a short period. If a person is more advanced, a guide can put them in a position to catch that memorable fish.

What is the key to catching big fish on the Bighorn?

More often than not, the key is good presentation. When that isn't working, an even better presentation. There is so much food, along with multiple conflicting currents, that if your fly isn't acting like the natural, it will get ignored time and time again. Another important key is understanding the water fish want to be in during each season. When the water is cold in the spring, a lot of fish are together. Smaller fish are going to be more competitive and beat big fish to the fly. Sometimes it's just picking through other fish to finally get to the bigger one. Other times it's patiently waiting and stalking the big fish when it finally shows itself. When the water is warmer and fish spread out, patience and observation pay off even more. Big fish can sit in out-of-the-way places, and you just have to spend time moving slowly and trying to pick them out visually before making any casts.

What advice would you give to anglers fishing "skinny water" or sight-fishing on the Bighorn?

Observe a blue heron. It is the best fisherman on the river. It is drab-colored, doesn't make a lot of movement, and has the patience to stand and observe. Ditch the brightly colored shirts and hats. Wear natural colors so you blend into the surroundings better. Be patient and move slowly. Fish will see you, but more importantly hear you moving in the water long before you ever have the chance to see the fish. Observe, observe, observe. Scan the water multiple times and from different angles while moving slowly. Fish will start to stand out from their environment.

A good presentation is the most important ingredient for being successful on the Bighorn. Your ability to mend and manage your line well will often lead to success. PAUL RUHTER

What are your top fly patterns and why?

A sow bug is my number one fly. They are in the river every day of the year and trout will eat them whenever they can. It is almost always the top fly on my nymph rig. The Ray Charles and soft-hackle Ray Charles have been around for years but are still the sow bug patterns that work the best.

For dry flies, I like a cripple pattern for each hatch. The vast majority of insects do not hatch. They are crippled in some way or another and don't survive to become viable adults. Somehow fish know cripples are easy targets. Cripple patterns are effective on the front end of and during the hatch and even do well when there are mostly spent spinners on the water. I like to use Thor's Cripple for *Baetis*, PMDs, and Tricos. It's a simple, low-riding, and effective cripple pattern. For caddis, the X Caddis works well to mimic emerging and crippled caddis. Harrop's Transitional Midge is a great emerging/cripple midge pattern.

What are a few tips you would offer anglers about fishing the midge emergences in the spring?

Spring midges are one of the most demanding hatches. The bugs are small and the water is cold. This means a stocked fly box and precise casting are required for success. Another key to success is observing. Midge hatches don't stand out like mayfly or caddis hatches in that the hatching insects can be next to impossible to notice. You will see fish starting to rise near the surface, taking emerging pupae but not noticing bugs. Most people rush to put on a dry fly when this happens, when trailing a subsurface pattern is what's needed. Small drys that sit low in the film are effective once you see snouts starting to come out of the water but are difficult for anglers to see. A larger dry fly as an indicator works well but shouldn't be too obnoxious. The water is cold, around 39 to 41 degrees, which means the fish are not going to move right or left to take a fly. Your casting has to put a fly right in their feeding lane, which at the most is only about six inches wide.

What are some common mistakes you see anglers make?
When dry-fly fishing, what I call flock shooting. People start casting to different fish and then start casting to the top of the pod thinking if their fly goes through all those fish, one should eat it. However, they've spooked almost every fish in the pod. Take the time to make good casts and presentations. It's better to put down one or two fish in figuring out what's not working instead of putting down all the fish.

What is your favorite part about guiding?
People. I spent over twenty years sitting at a desk looking at a computer screen, and people were probably my least favorite part of the job. When I became a guide, that changed. I thoroughly enjoy the people I work with, work for, and get to take fishing. No deadlines, projects, or fires to put out. When you see full-grown adults laughing because they are having such a good time, it really makes your day.

Chad Pavlick

Having grown up in Billings, Montana, Chad was bred to be a Bighorn River fishing guide. He has guided since 1999 and is an independent outfitter for Kingfisher Lodge in Fort Smith.

What is the appeal of fishing a tailwater river versus a freestone river?
Tailwaters have consistent water conditions, hatches, trout populations, and more. For fishermen that only have so many days to fish a year, this is important. Timing the best fishing on a freestone river can be difficult if you are traveling from 2,000 miles away. No matter when you come to a tailwater such as the Bighorn, you can have good fishing.

Do you have advice for skinny water fishing, or sight-fishing?
Always look for a fish before you cast a fly! Learning to sight fish and spot fish in the river is an acquired skill and one that not many people who come to the Bighorn know how to do. Once you learn what to look for, it is amazing the variety of water you can see fish in. Also, by doing so, you begin to recognize feeding behavior in relation to the type of water you are fishing. You are not only looking for the fish, but distinguishing how that fish is feeding and what they are feeding on.

Choosing the right fly pattern will often result in the angler catching a few or many fish on any given day, such as this nice rainbow. JAY NICHOLS

Do you have advice on fly selection?

I don't have anything tricky or flashy, but I do change the color and silhouette throughout the season. I like to use simple, impressionistic patterns that represent insects in a generic fashion. The Quill Nymph and Pheasant Tail are prime examples of simple patterns that I use all year and I tie them slightly different based on what is hatching and the water conditions. As a guide, I am always making adjustments to my patterns season by season and year by year. All in all, your techniques should change more with the seasons rather than your fly patterns.

What are the advantages of hiring a guide?

With good guides you gain the advantage of time management. These guides know when and where to have their clients at any given time to make the most of the river conditions. They are on the water regularly and know the pulse of the river. This is even more important on a busy river such as the Bighorn!

Hiring a guide is not only for new anglers. A good guide can do wonders with an advanced angler that wants to use a particular technique that he/she likes to fish. There are many other ways to catch a fish on this river other than a standard indicator nymph rig, especially with the large number of trout per mile.

Do you have any tips for fishing the spring midge hatch?
The most important thing is picking the correct water for that particular day, based on water and weather conditions, and knowing when to fish on the surface or on the bottom. Pick a spot, and be ready for anything. You need to be versatile with your techniques. At times the fish will feed on larvae; other times they will feed just below the surface on pupae or on the surface to single adults or clusters. Be prepared to fish anything from indicator to dry-dropper to greased-line, depending on the conditions.

What are your thoughts on fishing from the boat versus wading?
A boat is a great tool to mend an angler's line and row their drift with the flow of the current. Wading always gives the angler instant feedback on whether their drift is good or bad because they need to make it happen on their own.

The key to catching fish on the Bighorn is doing both based on where the fish are holding and how they are feeding. Be prepared to mix it up! Wading gives you access to many overlooked spots that you wouldn't be able to fish from the boat.

Eric Wilcox

> *Eric was born to be one thing and one thing only—a fishing guide. His unique approach to the river makes him one of the most well-known guides in the valley. He guides for the Bighorn Angler in Fort Smith.*

How do you find good water for your clients when the river is crowded?
Always watch your options, and move when something better opens up. I am 100 percent confident that I can catch fish on water that has already been fished. The first guy through gets the dumb ones. The fish in the river want to eat. If I don't want to deal with the crowds, I go to the lower river, where there are far fewer people yet more fish than the best stretch of another river.

How can a good fly caster become a good fisherman?
Leave the fly in the water! Only a third of overall execution is your casting. The cast complements the presentation. Emphasis needs to be on your presentation. The cast is only the beginning.

The Bighorn is one of the most user-friendly rivers in the West. Its flows and bottom are very wadable and the water is relatively easy to read. HALE HARRIS

What is the importance of having the right pattern?

This is a river that gets sick of commercial fly patterns. Let your freak flag fly. Show them something different on highly pressured water. My patterns are different enough that I can go behind someone and show them something different than the next guy. Fish your best fly pattern to locate fish, then change it up to catch more of them. Patterns should evolve with insects. Patterns are not always en vogue at a certain time, but always have a place and will again. My patterns are dictated by what is in the trout's stomach.

What are your concerns for the Bighorn moving into the future?

Water. Wyoming has got to realize that it's not just their water. Water is all relative to the lake. The lake dictates how the river is allowed to behave. The fish are the beneficiaries of good flows. Consistency of water temperature dictates life in the river and the stability of it. Fish need more water at certain times of the year. Bump scouring flow scheduled every year, like every freestone. We can afford it—there is enough water.

What are the keys to being a successful streamer fisherman?

Casting ability and distance—the longer the retrieve, the more water you cover. Persistence is also important. Apply a cast consistently and establish a pattern in your presentation. Streamer fishing can be the most technical application of the fly. You are imitating a larger organism that has a more complicated life. Apply different technique at all times.

What is the place of the Bighorn River in the grand scheme of great trout-fishing rivers?
It is a perfect blend of a river mated with a spring creek. It is resilient—it remains constant and fertile. Water is what makes it resilient. Bighorn Lake is the mother; the river is its breath, its blood. It needs to be recognized. It is so giving, yet abused through neglect for water.

What has changed?
Fishing practices have changed over the years. I see poor ethics constantly where anglers forget principle for personal gain. In a nutshell, crowding fellow anglers and, most importantly, shuffling—there's a reason why they call it crotch walking. May the fleas of a thousand camels infest a shuffler where it itches.

Richard Montella

Richie grew up in New Jersey fishing many of the famous waters of the East. After one trip to the Bighorn, he quickly moved West. Richie started guiding the river in 1982 and is known around town as "The Legend" for good reason.

How much does an angler need to know about insect hatches to be successful on the Bighorn?
You don't need to know that much. To catch them, you need to know what the fish are eating at a given time, as well as when and how they are eating it. You also need to imitate the natural and present it properly. Proper presentation adds up to numbers of strikes.

What skills are necessary for being an effective dry-fly angler?
The most important is casting accuracy. Not distance—you can approach these fish from the back and get close. Sometimes across, but most often you are fishing up to the fish, which allows you to get close.

You have been fishing and guiding on the river for over thirty years. How have you seen the insect hatches change over your fishing career on the Bighorn and why?
During high-flow years the hatches are less intense and primary insects get washed out. More consistent flows with fewer extremes produce more consistent hatches. Because of sustained low flows, we no longer have craneflies or Golden Stones like we used to, and hatches such as Yellow Sallies were gone for a while but now have come back. We used to have bigger bugs and the hatches were longer in duration.

Many anglers don't put enough pressure on the fish after setting the hook. Change the angle of your rod and put maximum pressure on the fish to land them quickly.
PAUL RUHTER

What advice would you give an angler about fighting fish?
Keep putting pressure on the fish—enough pressure where you don't break the leader, but you want to make the fish commit. The angler needs to control the fight and lead the fish with side pressure, pulling it side to side. Get the line on the reel as quickly as possible, so you don't get tangles in the line.

How do water flows and angler pressure affect the size and density of trout populations on the Bighorn?
Angling pressure changes the behavior of fish. The trout get warier. As an angler, you need to show these fish something different than what they have seen over and over. Low flows cause poor food in the winter, and when this happens, big fish eat small fish. Big fish become harder to catch with more pressure. Fish aren't in the heads of runs and/or shallows because anglers move them.

What are common mistakes anglers make when fishing nymphs?
When wade fishing, anglers need to adjust their weight for the run they are fishing. Make small adjustments. Most fish too light of weight. Most fish move into water along the edge of the river where it is efficient to feed when insects are emerging. People are often standing on the fish.

In all the years that you have been fishing the Bighorn, do you have a most memorable year and why?
I've always had fantastic fishing each year, so its hard to say. But in 1987 we had a hatch of cicadas. One day I was guiding two guys that had six hours to fish. We floated from Afterbay to Bighorn without stopping. We caught 188 fish on big dry flies, with many in the 4- to 5-pound range.

The biggest fish I ever personally caught was a male rainbow. I hooked it in fast water on a Golden Stone near the Colorado Club, and it broke me off. I came back two days later and hooked him again with the same nymph, finally landing him a few hundred yards downriver. He was 13 pounds, 8 ounces. I was using 0X. I got my fly back from when he broke me off a few days before.

What makes for a good client, and what can a client do to make the most of a guided trip?

Cooperation with the guide. Listen to the guide: he will tell you what to do to make the most of the day. Clients should be open to learning, not just catching fish. The guide has the expertise. Once you learn proper technique, then you will catch fish and be able to apply that technique when fishing by yourself without a guide.

CHAPTER 10

The Future of the Fishery

Since being opened to the public a little over thirty years ago, the Bighorn River has proved itself to be one of the country's premier trout fisheries, yet it is not without issues. In the coming decades, the Bighorn is bound to face many of the same challenges and management issues that it has faced over the past three decades. There will most likely be other new ones. Fortunately, the Bighorn River community is made up of anglers and organizations that are dedicated to protecting the river that we all love.

Since the trout fishery is the result of the construction of a massive concrete dam, the river itself changes little. Furthermore, the entire length of the trout fishery lies within the confines of Crow Indian Reservation, which has protected the rivers bank from the encroachment of development seen on many of the more popular Montana trout rivers.

While the structure of the river has remained relatively unchanged, the angling pressure imposed upon the resource has increased. In 2005, the Bighorn River received 90,000 angler-use days, which almost doubled to 170,000 use days in 2011.

Seventeen years ago, George Kelly wrote in *Seasons of the Bighorn*, "Of much greater concern to me is the number of anglers who fish the Bighorn. The river has withstood this increasing pressure remarkably well, but one wonders how long it can do so." Luckily, nearly two decades later, I can report that the river still handles the increased angling pressure amazingly well. High angler satisfaction surveys and the number of anglers who return each year are the best indicators of this. With cooperation by anglers who share this public resource and the practice of proper river etiquette, we can expect that the Bighorn is well prepared to absorb the increased angling pressure that it will most likely have over the next two decades to come.

With angling pressure being the main concern of most anglers on the Bighorn, and throughout all of Montana, I feel that the availability and management of water, contained within the Bighorn River drainage, are

The sustainability of the Bighorn River fishery depends on many interest groups coming together to work toward a common goal. The Bighorn River Alliance provides a voice for anglers. HALE HARRIS

going to determine the fate of the river's fishing. Montana Fish, Wildlife & Parks biologists recommend a minimum flow in the river of 2,500 cubic feet per second. When this minimum flow is met or exceeded, the river has ideal conditions for successful spawning of Bighorn trout, along with conditions that promote healthy populations of invertebrates throughout the river. However, except during the highest of water years, this recommended flow is rarely met throughout the year. Regardless, the river seems to fish quite well at lower flows, just not as well as it potentially could if minimum flows were met or even exceeded.

The fate of river flows is not entirely in the hands of river managers, but rather Mother Nature. When snow falls in the mountains at an above-average rate, filling the reservoir, and spring rains rejuvenate the river, ideal conditions for both trout and aquatic insects occur. Unfortunately, throughout Montana since the start of the twenty-first century, Mother Nature has dictated a situation that produces below average flows more often than not. Therefore, managers are forced to do their best with the water that they have to work with.

The Bureau of Reclamation manages the outflows from the Bighorn Lake. With the power generated by the massive turbines at the base of the dam the bureau's top priority, outflows into the river are rarely directly influenced by the angling community. Any management in flow that is put into effect by the bureau on behalf of the fishery is a result of recommendations made by Montana FWP biologists. It's the job of the

Even with increased angling pressure, the future of the Bighorn Fishery is bright thanks to concerned anglers and groups such as the Bighorn River Alliance. JAY NICHOLS

angling community to act in cooperation with FWP biologists to gain influence with the Bureau of Reclamation.

Complicating the matter even further, Bighorn Lake lies within two states: Montana and Wyoming. Residing 70 miles from Yellowtail Dam is Horseshoe Bend, the main boat launch used by boaters to access Bighorn Lake for recreation. It is the main priority of lake users in Wyoming to keep more water in Bighorn Lake to make launching a boat easier at Horseshoe Bend, whereas it is the priority of river users in Montana to reduce lake levels to have the higher river flows necessary for a healthy trout fishery. While cooperation between the two sides has been tenuous, advocacy groups and concerned citizens on both ends of the lake have been working together to find management solutions that would appease both sides.

In 2007, the Bighorn River System Issues Group was formed by the Bureau of Reclamation to identify, explore, and recommend alternative courses of action to local, tribal, state, and federal entities responsible for managing the Bighorn River system resources as part of a long-term management strategy. It was formed because these entities were concerned that the Bighorn River system was not being managed in a way that fully protects and uses the system's resources to address the multiple demands, needs, and expectations of the public. The challenge is finding an appropriate balance between the public benefits of the resource, such as fishing, while recognizing the respective agencies' responsibilities and needs.

Influencing dam managers to make adjustments in management of flows is a difficult task, with the fishery as healthy as it is. Even with below average flows, from a trout population standpoint the river is as healthy as could be. Who could argue with the current trout populations of 7,500 fish per mile in the upper reaches of the river?

While the trout population per mile is rather high, increased sedimentation in the river has been a huge problem in recent years. This is caused when the river endures several years of below average flows that are not high enough to push sediment through the river system. This thick layer of sediment covers the river's streambed, choking out populations of aquatic insects and reducing the availability of spawning gravel and the flows in the river's side channels. The lack of spring runoff to cleanse the streambed, like on freestone rivers, compounds the effects of sedimentation. Many wish that the Bureau of Reclamation would replicate this spring runoff on the Bighorn with a spring "flush," when dam managers for a short period of time—usually 48 hours—would increase flow to artificially recreate what would have occurred naturally if the dam had not been built.

By reducing winter flows slightly, I feel that a flush could be achieved more frequently and could significantly increase the productivity of the river. In the early 2000s, during the most significant drought in recent history, the river lost its diversity of aquatic insects because immense sedimentation choked out all but the most prolific hatches. Fortunately, the

Maintaining a healthy minimum flow is the key to the health of the Bighorn River fishery and vital to keeping enough water in the river's side channels. HALE HARRIS

Bighorn is incredibly resilient. In 2009, the Bighorn saw its first high-water year after nearly a decade of drought. This significant increase in flow was able to flush the years of sedimentation downriver, and the diversity of hatches quickly returned. Anglers can expect this cycle to continue well into the future. Based on current management practices, we don't know what conditions and what hatches we're going to get from one year to the next. In my opinion, we need to find a way to manage the compounding effects of sedimentation, even during low-water years, for the health of the river and the fishery. We also need to find ways to maintain the minimum flow of 2,500 cfs in the river as recommended by Montana FWP.

Other problems are also important to address, such as loss of native plants being choked out by invasive species, increased nitrogen and chemical levels entering the river via irrigation returns carrying fertilizer, and new issues from increasing angling pressure.

Fortunately, there are many individuals, government agencies, and organizations working together as stewards of the watershed. Members of the Crow Indian Reservation, National Park Service, Montana FWP, Bureau of Reclamation, Bighorn River Alliance, and many anglers who love the Bighorn have worked to ensure the sustainability of the Bighorn River fishery for years to come.

The Bighorn River Alliance (bighornriveralliance.org) was formed in 1995 to protect, preserve, and enhance the river's fishery, and it has become the voice of anglers, from every generation, on the Bighorn River. The alliance is dedicated to protecting the health and vitality of the river, along with the interests of anglers, and regularly interacts with the Montana FWP and Bureau of Reclamation to ensure that the needs of Bighorn River stakeholders are heard. I highly recommend becoming a member.

Doug Haacke has worked tirelessly and cooperatively with every one of these groups and organizations to help protect and enhance the Bighorn River trout fishery. We all owe him and the many others a big and resounding "thank you." Here, Doug and I discuss many of the issues facing the Bighorn River today. For further information you can visit Doug's website at bighornriver.org.

Many anglers work together to help protect the Bighorn and its resources. Doug Haacke has emerged as a champion for the river, ensuring that future generations will have access to great fishing. JAY NICHOLS

When and why did you get involved with the Bighorn?

I have been a longtime member of the local Trout Unlimited chapter here in Billings, which mostly focused on the Yellowstone and smaller freestone rivers in our area, along with the Bighorn. I started getting more seriously involved in 2005, when I was appointed to the citizen advisory council of Montana Fish, Wildlife & Parks. Coincidently in 2005, the superintendent of Bighorn Canyon National Recreation Area sent out a letter to the Bureau of Reclamation and Montana FWP about cutting flows on the Bighorn. There was a town hall meeting scheduled in Lovell, Wyoming, to discuss the flow change addressed in the letter. I accompanied Montana FWP biologists and a FWP commissioner to this meeting. Other interested parties were there also, including the superintendent of Bighorn Canyon National Recreation Area and the powers that be at the Bureau of Reclamation. We pulled up to the meeting place, and there was a pickup truck in the parking lot with a banner on it that read "Keep Wyoming Water in Wyoming." The attendees were rather hostile and wanted Montana attendants to leave. We stayed, but later walked out when it became apparent the folks in Lovell were only concerned with shutting off flows to the Bighorn River.

Dam managers were there trying to educate attendees on how management of water throughout the basin needed to be managed for all stakeholders. Every thirty minutes, someone from Wyoming would re-state the need for flows to be cut to the river. Their views were blatantly one-sided. Toward the end, Wyoming representatives officially presented the Bureau of Reclamation with a request to immediately drop flows to 1,000 cfs. And of course all of this was over people's ability to more easily launch boats at Horseshoe Bend Access on the Wyoming side of the lake. Engineers and managers continued to present evidence of why this wasn't possible, which fell upon deaf ears.

This is when I realized how big and eminent a problem there was, and that flows could potentially be dropped to historic low levels that would be highly detrimental to the fishery. I took this information back to the angling community in Montana, and to the river advocates in Fort Smith especially, and made everyone aware that something needed to be done and people needed to get involved. Flows at this time were already 1,300 cfs because we were in the midst of a string of drought years; dropping it to 1,000 cfs would have only made things worse. At first, it was as if I was Chicken Little running through the streets shouting, "The sky is falling!" No one believed the folks in Lovell were crazy enough to ask for such a thing, nor Reclamation reckless enough to go through with it. At that point, I started the Friends of the Bighorn River website, and with the encouragement and expertise of Hale Harris and Steve Hibers at the Trout Shop, and the stalwart support of Montana FWP and our TU chapter, used the website and my technical skills to get the word out and start educating folks on how the river was being managed by Reclamation. Rather quickly, people were receptive, got involved, and the Montana side started to fight back. I have been working on water flow issues and all issues pertaining to the Bighorn River ever since.

I am still a member of the citizen's advisory council for Montana FWP. I sit on the board of the Bighorn River Alliance, am currently chairman of Montana Trout Unlimited, and serve as conservation director for Magic City Fly Fishers, the Billings TU chapter.

What is the minimum flow for the Bighorn to be a healthy river?

Ken Frazer, a fisheries biologist with FWP who has worked the Bighorn for thirty years, and who is a real hero of mine, always says, "The more water, the more fish. Period." At 2,500 cfs, all the side channel habitat so important for spawning and rearing is wetted. At 2,000 cfs, half of the side channel habitat is lost, recruitment of younger trout is reduced, and predation on younger fish by older fish increases. At 1,500 cfs, all side channel habitat is lost, and spawning and rearing is reduced to the main channel of the river. In all cases, flows below 2,500 cfs result in reduced populations of fish.

So low flows only affect spawning and rearing?

Low flows affect more than just recruitment. Low flows generally mean less sediment transport throughout the river system, which means diminished or even absent aquatic insect hatches. This affects food production for the fish and diminishes dry-fly fishing opportunities. Furthermore, low flows cause the mouths of the side channels to "armor," or build up with sediment and cobble, which in turn become quickly overgrown with vegetation (and more often than not invasive species such as Russian olive and salt cedar), which accelerates the choking off of the side channels. Long periods of low flows will see side channels disappear, and compaction of sediment which is much more difficult to flush when normal flows return. Low flows also make it much easier for sunlight to reach the river bottom, which is a requirement for algae growth and the reason you'll see much nastier algae blooms in low water and high sunlight years. Finally, nitrogen gas super saturation, when a phenomenon in atmospheric nitrogen is entrained in the water as the result of water plunging into itself, such as the case of a waterfall or tailwater sluice gate, is a bit more of a concern in low-water years.

You hear anglers constantly talking about flushing flows. Is a flush really that big of a deal?

Without a doubt, flushing flows that mimic a natural runoff or freshet help the fishery. Wyoming Fish and Game credit a high-volume, short-duration flushing flow to the fabulous recovery of the Bighorn River above the dam in Wyoming. A flushing flow every other year, or at an absolute minimum once every three years, would help to drastically reduce the effects of sedimentation. If we don't have a flush for several years, naturally or

Horses frequent the river's edge throughout the length of the Bighorn. HALE HARRIS

artificially created sediment that doesn't remain wet turns to cement and becomes that much more difficult to move through the system. The sediment prevents the completion of the life cycle of many of the river's aquatic insects, which are important not only for food but also for spectacular insect hatches. The length of the flush period and amount of water needed varies, but twenty-four-hour flushes of 6,000 cfs or higher, done routinely every year (or at least once every two or three years), will certainly help.

Who has final say on the management of water throughout the basin?
Make no mistake about it: the Bureau of Reclamation is steering that ship. They are *mandated* by Congress to manage the reservoir for hydropower, irrigation, and flood control. They are *asked* to manage the reservoir for recreation. This is an important distinction. When push comes to shove, recreation will always be a lesser priority. That being said, Reclamation states they try to take into account all stakeholders when devising or implementing water policy. Keep in mind stakeholders include water rights and contract, tribal interests and compacts, irrigators, flood control, National Park Service, Corp of Engineers, Western Area Power Administration, Montana FWP, and many, many others. The Bighorn Issues Group was formed by Reclamation so that stakeholders from all interests could have a voice (but not necessarily a vote).

Is the Issues Group effective?
While the group, which is open to the public, is a wonderful forum for expressing concerns about water management, it's more for show. By that,

I mean it looks to the folks in Washington like the Montana Area Office is genuinely concerned with river interests, when in fact in all the years of meetings with the Issues Group, one can point to only a small handful of changes that have occurred as a result.

What steps do you feel can be taken by managers of the watershed to protect the trout and the fishery?

I'm going to toot my horn and that of FWP's and point to one of the few successes we've enjoyed: the implementation of rule curves. Rule curves are a sophisticated set of algorithms that manage river releases over a period of time. In essence, it takes knee-jerk reactions and political influence out of the water management equation, and manages river releases based on historic precedence and current inflow forecasts. You see, in prior years, area managers were prone to manage the river too conservatively. One year, a drought year, we actually had flooding downstream because an area manager was not willing to accept that the snow in the mountains would melt. By his own admission, was over two million dollars in hydropower revenues lost that year.

Anyway, Reclamation water managers have been operating under the rule curves during the months of April through July with pretty good success. The folks in Wyoming are happy as can be, and those of us in Montana want to see the rule curves expanded to the entire year. Currently the rule curves require that the starting lake elevation in April be 3,617 feet, which makes it somewhat impossible to ever achieve flows over 2,500 cfs if you work out the flows for the rest of the year because you're always chasing that lake elevation which is—but shouldn't be—seemingly set in stone.

Rule curves aside, the entire Bighorn basin, which includes Boysen and Buffalo Bill Reservoirs, needs to be managed as a whole. The cooperation between these facilities has improved a great deal in the last few years, but I do believe more timely communication between the three would help, especially in low-water and extreme high-water years.

How do extreme flows or fluctuations in flows affect the fish themselves?

High flows (more water) don't have nearly the detrimental effects that low flows do, at least on the fishery, and the fishing can be very good. Fluctuating flows, especially during the spawn, can be a huge deal, however. One year, a Reclamation manager dropped the flows out from under spawning brown trout and an entire age class of fish was completely lost. Fortunately, the following year's spring had abundant moisture and the next age class filled in the gap with astounding speed, so we dodged a bullet that year.

Storms can occur at any time on the Bighorn; in this case swirling winds created a dust storm above Grey Cliffs.

What can be done to improve the fishing?

I was always taught that if you manage the fishery, the fishing will take care of itself. Of course, that's absolutely true, and that was my mantra until I started doing a little guiding. When you find out you're booked with some dudes who expect to find three days of epic dry-fly fishing, you start thinking about flushing flows and cleaning algae off hooks, size and numbers, and all sorts of things that the casual angler doesn't. Back-to-back big-water years means 10,000 trout per mile and lots of 14-inch fish in the net. Low-water years mean a lot fewer fish, and maybe skinny fish, but a few real bruisers. One thing the typical Bighorn angler doesn't know is that the average fish mortality on the river runs about 40 percent, which is a stunning number when you put a pencil to it—40 percent of the population leaves the system every year. That's why when you have a year like 2012 when *Saprolegnia* fungus killed so many browns, the fishery and the fishing improved afterwards. It's a real testament to the productivity of the Bighorn and what an amazing fish factory it can be. Anyway, I still believe that with sound water management, the fishing will take care of itself.

Do those muddy tributaries hurt the river?

It depends. There's not a lot that can be done about the mud coming in from several of the larger tributaries, especially Soap Creek. Many agencies have looked at mitigating the silt that comes in, but the nature of the soil and geography are such that nothing can be done. However, the irrigation return is something different. That return is often highly nutrified and warm and can result in unwanted algae growth and diminished oxygen saturation. Several conservation organizations are involved in projects to create concentrated wetlands near the river that will remove much of the nutrients from that water as well as cool it before it returns to the system.

What can anglers do to get involved in protecting the Bighorn River?

Join local organizations such as the Bighorn River Alliance, Magic City Fly Fishers, and larger organizations such as Montana Trout Unlimited that work to protect and enhance the Bighorn River. Education and awareness are the keys. Anglers should become educated about their fishery, remember these issues when they go to the polls, and vote for politicians that care about these concerns.

CHAPTER 11

Wyoming's Bighorn River

While anglers from around the world flock *en masse* each year to
fish the famous stretch of the Bighorn River outside of Fort
Smith, Montana, the Bighorn River in Wyoming remains in
relative obscurity. A respectable trout stream in its own right, the Bighorn
River in Wyoming offers quality fishing worth consideration by anglers.

This section of the river, flowing through Thermopolis, Wyoming, has
remained off the radar of anglers, mainly because of its isolated location in
regard to major airports, urban centers, or other prominent trout
destinations. The closest airports can be found in Cody, Jackson Hole, or
Casper, Wyoming, or Billings, Montana. All of these lie ninety minutes to
two and a half hours away. From Fort Smith, Montana, there is no direct
route through the Crow Indian Reservation, and a trip to Thermopolis
takes about four hours.

Separated by the 70-mile Bighorn Lake, the Bighorn River in Montana
and the Bighorn River in Wyoming share a few similarities but are
considered two different rivers by the anglers who fish both. The Bighorn
River starts in Wyoming as the Wind River, flowing down out of the
mountains of the same name. The Wind River Indian Reservation contains
the Wind River in its entirety. As it makes its way out of the mountains, it
flows northeast into Boysen Reservoir. After flowing over Boysen Dam, the
river flows through Wind River Canyon for approximately 15 miles before
leaving the Wind River Reservation and becoming the Bighorn River. The
Wind River Canyon is a solid trout fishery, offering the best angling
opportunity in the area. However, access to the canyon is difficult and
wading treacherous. A license from the Wind River tribe is required to
wade fish here, and floating this water is not permitted by license holders
unless accompanied by a guide from the one outfitting operation permitted
to do so.

The Wind River becomes the Bighorn River at the Wedding of the
Waters, just after leaving the Wind River Reservation. There is no
"wedding of the waters" here; in actuality, it is the marrying of two

The Bighorn in Wyoming is the product of a top-release dam, which produces a shorter fishing season than the Bighorn River below Yellowtail Dam in Montana. A healthy fishery exists nonetheless. JAY NICHOLS

names. Early settlers from this region of Wyoming originally named this section of the river the Wind River, while the same river, in what is now known as Montana, was called the Bighorn River. With two established names for the same river, in time it was decided that the stretch of water upriver of Wedding of the Waters would be known as the Wind River, and downstream from this point the river would be known as the Bighorn River.

From the Wedding of the Waters, good trout fishing can be found for approximately 25 miles, as the Bighorn winds its way through irrigated agricultural land, cliff walls, and thermal features toward the town of Worland. Throughout this section of river, anglers will find healthy populations of rainbow trout, brown trout, and cutthroat trout, which are not found in the Montana stretch. Rainbow trout make up the bulk of the fishery by far.

Like the Bighorn in Montana, this section is classified as a tailwater river. However, Boysen Dam is a top-release dam, where water comes off the top of the lake, the opposite of the Yellowtail Dam in Fort Smith, Montana. Top-release dams provide far less consistent fishing than bottom-release tailwater rivers, because they don't regulate water temperature throughout the year. Water coming off the top of the dam is significantly warmer, which causes the timing of everything from spawning to hatches to happen earlier in the year. In general, everything happens earlier here than on the Bighorn in Montana.

The Bighorn here is smaller—about two-thirds the size of the Bighorn in Montana. Flows typically range anywhere from 500 cfs to 1,500 cfs during the prime part of the season from April through June, except during high-water years, when flows in the spring can range from 2,000 to 5,000 cfs. I compare the Bighorn in Wyoming to a cross between the Bighorn River in Montana and the Bitterroot River in western Montana. Since the river goes through the Wind River Canyon after coming out of the dam, before turning into the Bighorn, the water from here down feels like a cross between a freestone and a tailwater river.

Sedimentation is also a much more significant factor with top-release dams such as Boysen Dam. Because of sedimentation in the Wyoming stretch of the Bighorn, successful spawn rates are significantly lower. Unlike the Bighorn in Montana, trout populations on the Wyoming stretch have to be supplemented with annual stockings by Wyoming Fish and Game. Each June, fisheries managers stock the section of the river from Wedding of the Waters down to Black Mountain Road access with approximately 8,000 cutthroat trout and 16,000 rainbow trout, which supplement wild trout populations during years of low recruitment.

Float fishing is the best way to prospect for trout in the lower stretches of the Bighorn in Wyoming. JAY NICHOLS

While there are not as many fish per mile in this stretch of the Bighorn, the average size is slightly larger for the brown, rainbow, and cutthroat trout present. JAY NICHOLS

In the best stretch of water, from Wedding of the Waters to Hot Springs State Park, trout populations are as high as 3,000 fish per mile, with populations gradually falling the further downriver you get. While the number of trout per mile in this stretch is fewer than the Montana stretch, on average they are slightly larger, often in the 16- to 17-inch range.

The Bighorn River is open to angling year-round. With varying water temperatures produced by Boysen Dam, this section of the Bighorn does not fish as consistently as the Bighorn in Montana. Most anglers visiting the Bighorn River in Wyoming do so in the first half of the year, before water temperatures become too warm. According to Thermopolis-based fishing guide John Schwalbe of Wyoming Adventures, who has been fishing and guiding this stretch of the Bighorn for over twenty years, April through early June offers anglers the best fishing conditions of the year. During this timeframe, optimal water temperatures conducive to intense insect emergences are reached much earlier than on the Montana stretch of the Bighorn. Anglers will be greeted by actively feeding trout that do so consistently above and below the surface.

The river will start fishing well in February. By this time midge hatches have already started, and fish will feed on these small but abundant morsels freely below the surface. Intense midge emergences will continue into March. Be prepared with a wide variety of larva and pupa imitations. Red Stretch Tube Larva, Zebra Midges, Root Beer Midges, RS-2s, and Black Beauty Emergers will all take fish.

By mid-March, strong Blue-Winged Olive emergences will begin and will last for nearly two months. During this time you will find fish readily feeding on the surface. Just like the Montana stretch, this section of the river has an incredible abundance of these size 18 to 20 mayflies. Fish will also feed on BWO nymphs throughout the day below the surface. Black Quills, Killer Mayflys, Wonder Nymphs, and Pheasant Tails will take trout below the surface. Be prepared to see fish feeding on the surface in the early afternoon along the edges of riffles and in back eddies. A good drag-free presentation with a CDC Sparkle Dun, Sipper Emerger, Thorax Dun, or Parachute imitation will take fish continually. By mid-May, water temperatures have increased significantly and the BWO hatches come to an end.

Scuds and sow bugs are also important in this stretch of the Bighorn, and throughout the spring imitations of both of these crustaceans will be just as effective as your midge larvae and BWO nymphs. It is best to fish a crustacean imitation above a midge or BWO pattern all spring. Ray Charles, Poxyback Sow Bugs, Firebead Sow Bugs, and orange and pink scud patterns all work well.

By the end of May, water temperatures are already hovering around 60 degrees in this section of the river. On the Montana stretch, we normally wouldn't see temperatures that high until mid-July. Because of the accelerated water temperatures, the Bighorn River in Wyoming sees summerlike fishing conditions toward the end of May and early June, signaled by Trico hatches two to three months earlier than you will find them on the Montana stretch of the Bighorn. Prolific emergences and dense spinner falls of these small mayflies will peak by mid-June, and then trickle off throughout the summer.

Coinciding with the Trico emergence is the start of the terrestrial fishing season. Some of the most exciting dry-fly fishing of the year can be had here with terrestrial insects such as flying ants and grasshoppers. I have had terrific terrestrial fishing as early as May. June is a prime month

Pete displays a thick brown trout that ate a Blue-Winged Olive dun pattern in one of the river's back eddies.

for hopper fishing and will last as long as water temperatures remain cool enough. Don't be afraid to incorporate movement into your terrestrial patterns on this section of the Bighorn. Movement on your fly will often elicit vicious strikes here. Carry grasshopper patterns with a wide variety of body colors and a few staple ant and beetle patterns. Anglers at this time may also encounter sporadic hatches of Pale Morning Duns, Yellow Sallies, and Tan Caddis. At certain times, fish will respond well to these naturals, both on and below the surface.

By July and August, water temperatures are at their upper threshold for a trout fishery. While July and August is prime time to fish on the Bighorn in Montana, due to the cold temperatures coming from the Yellowtail Dam, the opposite is true on the Wyoming stretch. At this same time, the growth of aquatic vegetation consumes the river, making it challenging to fish. Persistent anglers will find fishing opportunities early or late in the day and in fast-water riffles. Terrestrials and even craneflies will draw fish to the surface during these months. Most anglers at this time are fishing nearby freestone rivers or are spending most of their time in the Wind River Canyon where deep, boulder-strewn runs provide cold, well-oxygenated water for the trout.

By the end of September, the river begins to cool to more suitable water conditions. Anglers will find a great fall fishing window in September and October with hatches of Blue-Winged Olives that reach their prime in October, when water temperatures are again within an optimal range. Streamer fishing at this time will also become intriguing to anglers as brown trout prepare to spawn.

Terrestrials are a staple for anglers during the summer. Ants, beetles, and grasshoppers all produce fish if there are good water temperatures and flows. JAY NICHOLS

Access

Wade and float fishermen will find good access throughout the area, provided by both local municipalities and the state of Wyoming. Access laws in Wyoming differ from those in Montana. In Wyoming, the landowner not only owns the land adjacent to the river, but also the bottom of the river. You have to be cautious of where you walk and where you anchor your boat to make sure that you are not trespassing. Most of the best trout water from Wedding of the Waters to Hot Springs State Park is private. All in all, the Wyoming Fish and Game offers 13 miles of easements in which anglers can access the river.

The Wedding of the Waters is significant to anglers, since it is the first fishing access and boat put-in for this stretch. Located just a few short miles from the town of Thermopolis, this access offers a paved parking lot, concrete boat ramp, and wade-fishing access to walk-in anglers. From the Wedding of the Waters Access, you can float to the 8th Street Bridge in the center of Thermopolis (7 miles) or down to Hot Spring State Park (9 miles). This stretch produces the most consistent fishing and has the highest density of aquatic insects, the most fish per mile, and also the most traffic. Inside bends, riffles, seams, flats, and abundant side channels all provide optimal places to catch trout in this stretch.

The next stretch, from Hot Springs State Park to the Wakeley Fish and Game Access, is not a popular stretch due to the two significant diversion dams found throughout this stretch that are hazards to floaters. Wade access is also limited because of high cliff walls and private access. The water through here is also slow from being backed up by the diversion dams, which makes it not conducive to fly fishing. Anglers who fish this section of river will find a mix of browns and rainbows when conditions are right.

From the Wakeley boat ramp downstream, the river picks up speed once again and good fishing resumes. The river begins to widen throughout this stretch, and you will find productive runs in between long, slow flats, as well as plenty of riffles and drop-offs, along with side channels, that will be good places to cast a fly. Water temperatures should be taken into consideration before floating this section, especially during the summer. Anglers will find that the best luck down here is in the spring and fall, or in the evenings or early mornings during the summer. This is the last stretch of river that Wyoming Fish and Game stocks annually. Anglers will find predominantly rainbow trout throughout this stretch. From the Wakeley Boat Access, you can float 6 miles down to Longwell Boat Ramp, or another 2 miles to Skeleton Access. Unlike Longwell Access, which has a concrete boat ramp, the take-out at Skeleton is unimproved and may not be worth the trouble for some floaters. Between Wakeley and Skeleton there are also several walk-in fishing access sites that are marked off the main highway.

Blue-Winged Olives and Tricos, the predominant hatches here, bring nice browns like this to the surface. JAY NICHOLS

The density of insects in this stretch of river is lower than upstream, and fish down here will have a higher propensity to forage on larger food sources. Large trout will be found feeding opportunistically throughout this stretch on crayfish, leeches, and small baitfish. Blue-Winged Olives, Tricos, caddis, and craneflies will produce the best surface action here. Below this stretch of water, the river begins to warm significantly and irrigation returns cloud the river. A few trout persist as the river flows through the town of Kirby on its way to Worland, but it is rarely worth the effort.

Tactics and Rigs

Anglers can find success on the Wyoming stretch of the Bighorn with the same equipment and tactics used on the Montana stretch. Most anglers fish a double nymph indicator rig, set up similar to the rig I described for the Montana portion, but shorter to accommodate the river's size, depth, and features. Anglers should expect to set their strike indicator 5 to 7 feet from their split shot. Adjust your split shot based on the depth and speed of the water you are fishing. The fish will be sitting in different river features based on water temperature. The warmer it is, the more likely you will find fish under a shady bank or in a riffle rather than a slower run.

Nymphing a streamer under an indicator here can bring some large fish to the net. In addition to streamers, be prepared with other large subsurface imitations, such as crayfish, leeches, craneflies, and damselflies. Otherwise, anglers should expect to offer these trout the same diet of crustaceans, small mayfly nymphs, midges, caddis pupae, eggs, and worms as on Montana's tailwater.

Dry-fly anglers will find pods of fish in the many flats, along the edges of riffles, and in slack water along the banks. Match-the-hatch dry-fly fishing can be good in this section of river, and trout here will be willing to take your dry fly when presented properly. They are not especially leader-shy, but will only respond to a properly presented dry fly. Don't get too technical with your dry-fly patterns. All the standard imitations work well.

Streamer fishermen should be prepared with sink tip fly lines when stripping streamers and stout leaders when fishing them under a strike indicator, an ideal rig when the water is on the colder or warmer side of the optimal range and fish are less likely to move for or chase your imitation. In the spring and fall, when temperatures are ideal, stripping streamers can produce some exciting fishing. Streamer fishing can also be outstanding is right after runoff or when a "flush" occurs in this section. When the water is raised to simulate a spring runoff and force the river's sediment load downriver, the increased flow dislodges the river's leeches and crayfish, sending the trout into a feeding frenzy.

While fishing in this stretch is not as consistent as the Montana water, it can offer more diversity and the opportunity to use a wider array of tactics. A visit to this section of the river is worthwhile for those looking to explore new trout-fishing opportunities. A trip that encompasses a visit to both the Montana and Wyoming stretches of the Bighorn River is a doable option that I highly recommend to those who don't mind the drive time. The Montana and Wyoming sections of the river complement each other nicely.

The streamer fishing here is somewhat inconsistent, but when it's on, it can be good.
JAY NICHOLS

John Schwalbe, Thermopolis, Wyoming

John Schwalbe owns and operates Wyoming Adventures in Thermopolis, Wyoming. He has been guiding anglers on the Wyoming stretch of the Bighorn for over twenty years.

What advice would you give to a beginner when fishing the Bighorn?

The most important thing that I can teach beginners when they get in my boat is to just relax and listen. You never really know what a person's perception, mentality, or idea is when it comes to fly fishing. I have had a number of beginners that have an idea of what fly fishing is by watching *A River Runs Through It* and want to cast a hundred times before laying their line out. As a guide, I want my client to catch fish, have a fun day, and take some knowledge away when they leave. There are so many aspects to fly fishing that an angler must get down before they can become successful. This can be overwhelming to some. So at the start of the trip, before I even hand the fly rod to my client, I just have a conversation. I want to get them into the right mindset. This sets the tone for the day. It helps me to get the client where I need them to learn, and it allows the client to know my expectations for the day—to trust, listen, and to have fun.

What advice would you give to dry-fly anglers?

Watch your drift. The presentation of the fly is the most important facet to dry-fly fishing, even over fly selection, which is also important. Most of the time the fish are in slower-moving water where they have a chance to really check out the food they are consuming. They are zoned into a certain bug and they want it to look a certain way. It does not matter if you can cast a mile in beautiful form if you cannot present the fly to a sipping trout in a way that he likes.

What is the most important piece of equipment for where you fish?

I would say a drift boat. Due to the limited access to public water, a boat will enable anglers to cover more water, thus more fish. It will also allow them to get into areas that are not fished as much by wading fishermen.

What changes have you seen over the years on the Bighorn in Wyoming?

The most significant change is the amount of traffic. This stretch has been a well-kept secret for many years. With the influx of fishermen to the sport, social media, and guides in the surrounding areas bringing clients here, the number of anglers has increased drastically. For now, though, the crowds are seasonal and mostly on weekends and holidays. It is also relative. I understand what I call a busy day here is not what the guys in Fort Smith would.

Do you have a most memorable day of guiding, or one that stands out in your mind?

I'm lucky to say that over the last twenty-plus years as a guide I have been blessed with many days with clients that have been memorable and fishing that has been off the charts. One trip in particular was with a gentleman in his mid-seventies. He had been fly fishing his entire life and had fished all of the legendary Western trout streams. It was the perfect BWO day, with overcast and off-and-on spitting rain. There were stretches that you would look downstream and all you saw were snouts, backs, and tails. We threw drys all day to eager pods of feeding trout. Some were in such a feeding frenzy they could care less that you were pulling fish after fish out of the same pod. They just kept chowing. It was most anglers' ideal setting, and

Thermopolis, Wyoming

The main draw to Thermopolis is by no means fly fishing, but rather the thermal features contained within Hot Springs State Park. While this may be the case, Thermopolis makes for a suitable base of operations when fishing the Bighorn River in Wyoming. The river runs right through downtown, where you will find suitable restaurants, bars, hotels, gas, and groceries throughout your visit. What you won't find is a dedicated year-round fly shop. Canyon Sporting Goods and Thermopolis Hardware located on Highway 20 (the main drag) offer a few basic fly-fishing items and a place to buy fishing licenses, but you won't find specialized tackle or flies for the river. Wind River Canyon Whitewater has a small fly shop, but I have found it only conducts regular business hours during the summer season. Buying a license online before you arrive is your best bet. Thermopolis is slowly becoming more of an angler's town, as the Bighorn River here becomes better known. Thermopolis provides all the necessary amenities to complement this trout-fishing destination, and I would expect more services would be offered in the future as its popularity grows.

For current fishing information, it is best to contact a shop in one of the nearby fishing towns, such as Fort Smith, Montana, or Cody or Casper, Wyoming. The staff at the Bighorn Angler in Fort Smith, North Fork Anglers in Cody, or Platte River Fly Shop in Casper can provide you with up-to-date fishing information and suggested fly patterns to use for your visit.

Floating this section of the Bighorn with a guide is a great option, and several area-based operations provide guided fly-fishing trips in the area. John Schwalbe of Wyoming Adventures has been doing it for a long time, and his guides know the river well. The Bighorn Angler offers guided trips in the spring and fall, when fishing is at its best, as does Tim Wade's North Fork Anglers in Cody, Wyoming. ■

the man kept commenting on how he never had a better day of fishing. We caught countless fish, but the thing that stands out the most was just the youth in this man's demeanor. He acted as if he was twenty years old again. He was whistling and singing, and for several hours his mind was off of the aches and pains of life that come with age.

Favorite hatch or season on the Bighorn in Wyoming?

Tricos are my favorite hatch. They start at the end of May or first week in June when the water temperatures reach 62 degrees. The hatch will go throughout the fall, usually ending in mid-October when it gets too cold. In high-water years, the fish will not exert the energy to rise due to water pressure. However, since we are in a high plains desert, this only occurs once or twice every several years. The significant aspect of this particular hatch is the abundance of bugs on the water. This is especially true after the late-morning spinner fall occurs (the female duns begin hatching around sunrise).

What are your favorite fly patterns?

In the winter and spring, I often am using red midge pupae and sow bug patterns. I like to use any pattern that has a realistic look to it. I'm not a big flashy or beadhead guy. I like to serve up what the trout are keying in on. In the summer it gets mossy, so I stay to the surface. I like terrestrials, mostly hoppers. For this stretch of the Bighorn, a foam-bodied Joe's Hopper

Large, healthy rainbows such as this one draw anglers to waters near the town of Thermopolis.

will take fish at will, especially in good grasshopper years. The fall brings out BWOs more consistently than in the spring. If they are not feeding on the surface, then I like to use variations of Pheasant Tail–type nymphs. If they are on the surface, I like CDC flies and any pattern that is tied on a scud hook. This allows the fly to sit a bit deeper into the surface film. It just stands out a bit when the trout are scanning for their next morsel.

What mistakes do you commonly see anglers make?

Assuming that anglers have their casting down, the most common mistake I see is on the hook set. Often anglers set too slow or so hard and they must think they are in a bass tournament. Another common mistake is with the angle of the set. Anglers often pull the fly out of the trout's mouth when they should be making a side-arm set into the direction of the fish's open mouth. I see a lot of the opposite, which pulls the flies away from the trout.

If you could change anything about the Bighorn in Wyoming, what would it be?

I would start with the difficult task of educating people. Anglers need to understand the carnage they can leave behind due to ignorance. I see guys handling fish poorly. This can be from fighting them too long, keeping them out of the water for an exaggerated amount of time for pictures and often dropping them, or holding them with fingers in their gills. I see anglers walking through redds in the spring and fall and targeting the trout that are in the process of reproducing. I do not believe that it would be too much to ask for all fishermen to have to go through a course similar to hunters. This course could go over both boat safety and etiquette and fishing safety and etiquette. I would also look into changing slot limits, and wish there was more accountability through law enforcement. The Bighorn River is an amazing resource, and we have an obligation to take care of it. We must be more proactive.

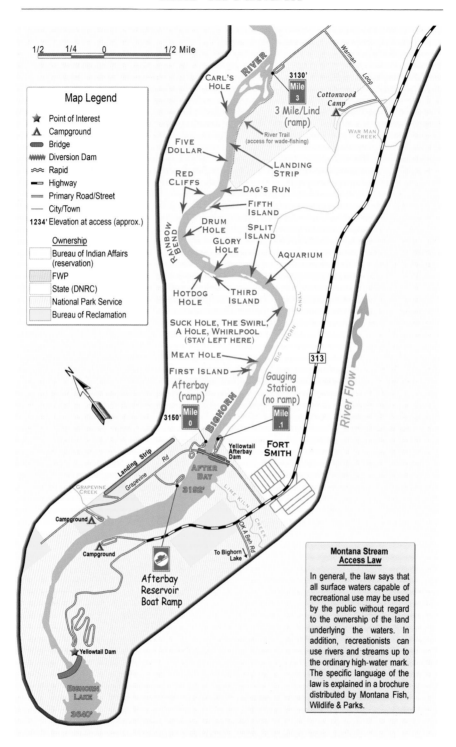

Map Legend

★ Point of Interest
▲ Campground
▬ Bridge
〰 Diversion Dam
≈ Rapid
━▭ Highway
═ Primary Road/Street
— City/Town
1234′ Elevation at access (approx.)

Ownership
Bureau of Indian Affairs (reservation)
FWP
State (DNRC)
National Park Service
Bureau of Reclamation

1/2   1/4   0   1/2 Mile

CARL'S HOLE
3130′ Mile 3
Cottonwood Camp
3 Mile/Lind (ramp)
Warman Loop
WAR MAN CREEK
River Trail (access for wade-fishing)
FIVE DOLLAR
LANDING STRIP
RED CLIFFS
DAG'S RUN
FIFTH ISLAND
DRUM HOLE
SPLIT ISLAND
RAINBOW BEND
GLORY HOLE
AQUARIUM
HOTDOG HOLE
THIRD ISLAND
BIG HORN CANAL
SUCK HOLE, THE SWIRL, A HOLE, WHIRLPOOL (STAY LEFT HERE)
MEAT HOLE
313
FIRST ISLAND
Gauging Station (no ramp)
River Flow
Afterbay (ramp)
3150′ Mile 0
Mile .1
BIGHORN
Yellowtail Afterbay Dam
FORT SMITH
Landing Strip
Grapevine Rd
AFTER BAY **3192′**
LINE KILN CREEK
GRAPEVINE CREEK
Campground ▲
Campground ▲
Afterbay Reservoir Boat Ramp
OK A Beh Rd
To Bighorn Lake
★ Yellowtail Dam
BIGHORN LAKE **3640′**

Montana Stream Access Law

In general, the law says that all surface waters capable of recreational use may be used by the public without regard to the ownership of the land underlying the waters. In addition, recreationists can use rivers and streams up to the ordinary high-water mark. The specific language of the law is explained in a brochure distributed by Montana Fish, Wildlife & Parks.

Afterbay—Three Mile Access

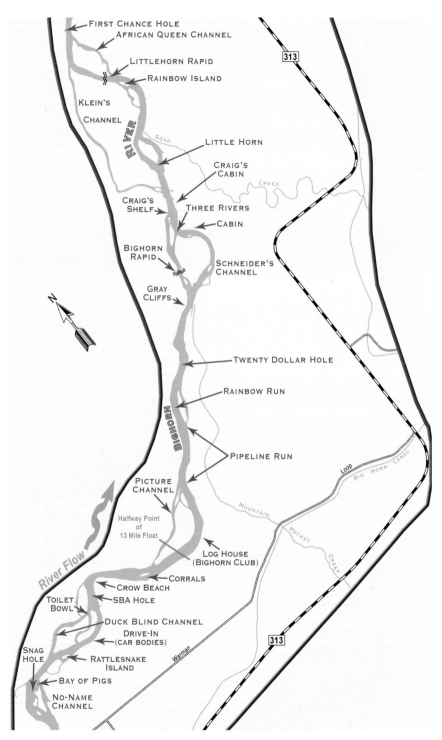

Three Mile Access—Bighorn Access

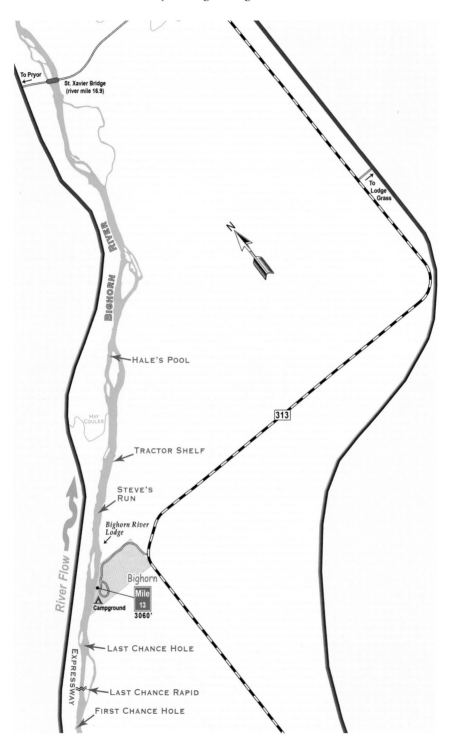

Bighorn Access—St. Xavier Bridge

St. Xavier—Mallard's Landing

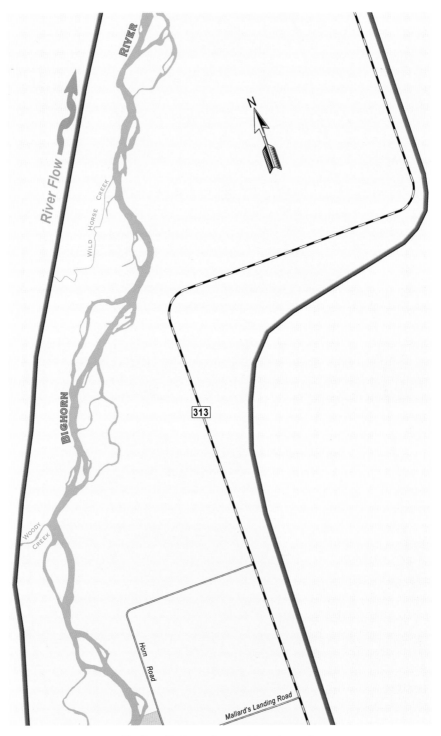

Mallard's Landing—Two Leggins

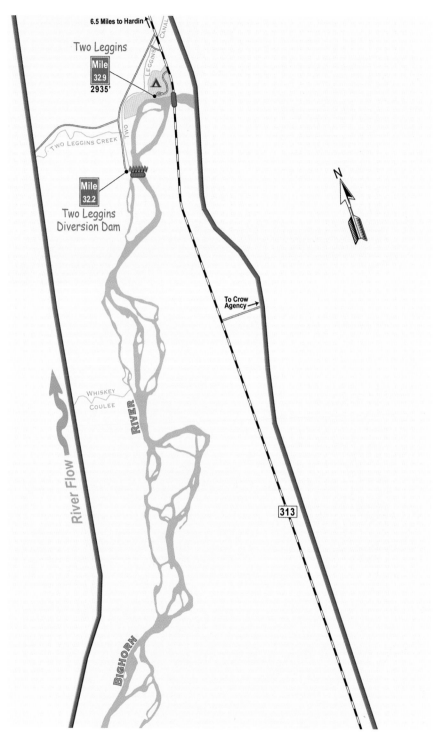

Mallard's Landing—Two Leggins (continued)

INDEX